World War 2

────── ❧❧❧❧❧ ──────

Waffen SS Soldiers
Testimonies of German SS Soldiers

2nd Edition

Oliver Mayer

The information herein is offered for informational purposes solely, and is universal as so. The presentation of the information is without contract or any type of guarantee assurance.

The trademarks that are used are without any consent, and the publication of the trademark is without permission or backing by the trademark owner.

All trademarks as well as brands within this book are for clarifying purposes only and are the owned by the owners themselves, not affiliated with this document.

Contents

Introduction

It was the year 1925 and Adolf Hitler was grooming a new breed of men. They were known as the 'Schutzstaffel," a German word that means protective echelon. This breed of men were to serve as Hitler's special bodyguards during his rise to power. They were referred to as the SS soldiers. With Hitler as the leader of the Nazi Party, and later, becoming the leader of Germany, these special soldiers were able to exercise incredible power, and illicit significant fear amongst the German people.

Under the leadership of Heinrich Himmler, the SS soldiers were given military training and psychological training, where they were taught to believe that they were the most superior beings in all human kind, especially as none of they had any Jewish ancestors.

As World War II begun, SS soldiers were 250,000 strong, covering a multitude of functions for Hitler. What they are most remembered for however is their cruel crimes during this war, and the terror that they spread throughout all of Germany and her borders.

This book contains testimonies from six SS soldiers who were active during World War II. It shall put you into the heart of their experiences, and describe what being a part of the most powerful organisation on earth (at that time) was like.

Chapter 1:

The Testimony of Heinz Fisch

T he year of my birth was 1921, and I was born a proud German. It was when I turned 18 that I thought to become part of Hitler's army, part of the SS. I thought that becoming a soldier would make me a better German, that it would prove my loyalty. When I thought of being a soldier, death, shooting and war was not what came to mind. Rather, I thought of marching, a smart uniform and national pride. In that, I believed I would prove myself honourable.

I met all the requirements, being Aryan in my ancestry, standing at 5 foot 11 inches and being 19 years of age. My family were in full support of my decision, and in fact, urged and pushed me to join Hitler's army. For them, it would have been a sign of prestige amongst peers, and proven that we were doing what we could as a family to help further the agenda of our mighty leader.

So I joined up and prepared to go through the training that was needed to get me in shape. To begin with, training involved learning a range of drills that could be used to face any situation, including what to do in case of a land mine, a bomb, a fire, flooding situations and much more. Following this, there was training on marching and staying in total order while in battle. Soldiers were expected to be neat and clean as much as possible, and disorganisation was not allowed. Following this I received my combat training, that taught me how to face opponents and fight them one on one. I completed my training and was officially a member of the SS. In was 1941 when I was told that I would be serving outside of Germany, in a concentration camp named Auschwitz, and I was made a member of the SS-Totenkopfverbande.

I was excited at the prospect of going to the camp, and helping to keep the Jews under control as we were at war. It seemed much less daunting that the front line, where all the 'action' was meant to be. In my mind, controlling those who threatened and dared to go against the Germans was sending a much stronger message than attempting to shoot enemies who quite often could not even see me. I wanted those who were against us to know who I was, and to have my face etched in their memories. I needed them to know that what I was doing was in loyalty to me leader.

At the camp, I was assigned my duties, which included daily patrols to make sure that there was no trouble in the camp. Every day, there would be Jews coming into the camp, and to say that I felt hatred towards them would be greatly undermining my feelings. I despised them, and I had always despised them. I did not even consider them to be human.

From the time that I had been in school, I had been taught about the evil of the Jews and all the reasons that they were not to be accepted amongst us puritans. I was glad when they had all been driven out of our village and the surrounding villages as well. Many times, whenever I would see a Jew I would feel triggered, and my entire body would fill up with rage.

I would keep watch as my comrades in arms would go through the selecting process, picking the healthy Jews to work, and putting to the side those that were not in good condition for some "special action". This was a term that had been used quite often, though I was trying to figure out what exactly it meant. What I did know was that it was a worthy punishment, and any Jew who would receive special action would never be able to repeat the mistake that they had made. When any of them would get out of line I would use the butt of my gun and push them back in line. It would take some time before I learned the real fate of the 'weaker' Jews, and even though I hated them, it took a while for me to fully accept.

I learned military songs, the ones that talked about Jewish blood and how their death would mean a better life for all. Together with the other SS soldiers in the camp, we would sing, eat and make merry when we were not working. We always made sure that we sang as loudly as possible, so that the Jews would hear the words of our songs. We wanted them to know what we were thinking, and there was no need to spare any thoughts for the feelings of people that we believed to be animals. We knew that our actions would break them down, and for me, that was a rewarding thought. Life for me, was actually quite present despite the war.

This all changed the day I found out what "special action" really meant. A new shipment of lot of Jews were being admitted into Auschwitz, and I happened to be guarding those that were not considered to be healthy. It was then that I overhead my comrades discuss how they were to be exterminated. The conversation appeared to be so light hearted, that I could barely believe what they were talking of. I was astounded by my own naïveté, and ignorance as to what was happening in the camp. Although I could admit to hating the Jews and being filled with rage, I could not find a way to justify within me the fate that awaited those who had arrived at the camp.

I tried to count how many Jews were to be finished off that day, and when I got to 132, and they continued to increase in number, I stopped. It was like becoming numb. I chose not to think about it, I chose to eliminate all consciousness and focus on my task at hand. I chose to freeze emotion. I arranged them all into the lines they were to follow as they walked into the gas chamber. I did my part, making sure that they had all stripped of their clothing and were dressed in the striped 'pyjamas' that were reserved for all prisoners. I collected and placed all their jewellery in the selected bin. I did all this like a robot, in the most functional way, and never once opening my mouth to say a word. I knew that if I had, my emotions would have given me away.

The Jews were led to the gas chambers alive, and removed from these chambers dead. All this happened in less than thirty minutes. In this time, there would be loud screams which would get softer and softer until they had stopped all together. I remember being glad that I did not have the job of piling up their bodies, though at times, I can still hear their screams in my head. Most of them would scream when they realised what was happening to them. Then they would bang against the walls of the gas chamber, as if doing so would create a miraculous opening through which they could escape. Escape was futile, all that was left for them was death.

I drank a lot during this time, and one night, I was called to action, even though I was in a mild stupor. As I followed my comrades I was led to the edge of the camp, where there were some Jews that had been lined up in a row. Around me were fellow soldiers, mocking the Jews, laughing at them, and making fun of their facial features. I joined in because it was funny to me at the time. I used to relish in the humiliation of the Jews. Then things took a turn that I did not expect. I was given the order to shoot at will, and kill as many as I would like. I remember my commanding office telling me that this was a reward for all my hard work.

Conscience seemed to wash over me, and at that moment, I would have given anything to take to my heels and run. My head which had been cloudy with alcohol and heady laughter seemed to clear up instantly, making me fully conscious of the decision that I was about to make and what I was about to do. In the back of my mind is what I call my 'German' voice, the one that would tell me I needed to remain loyal, to do what was best for Germany. I closed my eyes and lifted my rifle, and when I opened my eyes, I was lying down and around me was laughter. I had apparently fainted before I could even take a shot. I feigned shame while all the while I was thanking God for putting me in that condition.

It was just my luck that I was never called to do something like this again, and this made it easier for me to turn a blind eye to all that was happening. That is possibly how I managed to make it through this entire time. I spent my time doing guard duty, and skilfully managed to avoid being near the Jews who were being selected for the chambers. I went back to singing silly songs, having a few drinks (and making sure that I went to bed straight afterwards) and looking for activities and occurrences in the course of the day that would bring me joy.

Looking back, I know that I bear some responsibility for what happened to the Jews, but I find my own solace in the fact that I never used my own hand when it came to the killings. There is some guilt for being an observer, but at the time, there was nothing that I could do to change what was happening – not if I valued my own life. Now, I feel some shame, some of the time, but for the most part, I have made my peace. I accept that what occurred was simply life. It was simply the way life had to be.

Chapter 2:

The Testimony of Otto Gerbhardt

I remember the smoke that burned for days, when myself and other members of my SS Battalion were destroying the camp which we have been posted in. We were preparing to leave north-eastern Poland, where we had lived in a forest, and head back to the country where we were born, Germany.

I had been stationed at this camp for at least one year, after a period where we moved around constantly and were never in one place for more than two months. Due to this, the camp was like a second home, the place where we found rest and a base of operations. However, when you are at war you quickly learn not to form attachments to things or places as circumstances can change in an instant. It appeared that the war was coming to an end, and we were to leave no evidence of the camp, especially the activities that we have carried out. This was what we did to Treblinka.

Being located in such a remote area meant that for the most part, our camp was 'forgotten'. However, that did not mean that we were dormant in any way, we were incredibly active when it came to fulfilling our purpose, the purpose that we had been given by our leader, to do what was necessary to control the Jews. In addition to controlling them, we were also given the secret directive to eliminate them if necessary.

The camp was divided into two sections, Treblinka 1 and Treblinka 2. I was based in Treblinka 1. My part of the camp was where the Jews were put to work, as they were forced labour. The other part of the camp was where the Jews were put to death. It paid to be a strong Jew, preferably male, as this meant that your chances for survival were relatively high. Women were not lucky in this respect, especially those who had small children. They were more of a burden, or only good for experiments until they gave up on life themselves.

As SS soldiers, we gave the impression that both sides of the camp were the same, especially towards the prisoners who were in the side of the camp that I was working in. The last thing that we needed was for there to be some sort of uprising to the goings on. That is why it was impossible to see into the other camp, as the barbed wire fence that separated both sides was covered with branches that completely blocked the vision.

To get to the core of the second camp, where the Jews were being killed, you would have had to walk for just over a kilometre. This distance meant that the sounds of screams or anything similar would never be heard at the first camp. Even if anything was heard, it would be incredibly muffled and impossible to discern.

Most of the prisoners that we controlled for labour were Polish, as well as being Jewish. They had the heavy job of unloading the trains that carried freight into the station at Treblinka. Other jobs including cutting down trees to make room for buildings and for roads. This was one advantage of being a soldier in the army, it was possible to delegate all the heavy tasks, and simply oversee the actions being taken.

Sometimes I would be put on guard duty near the entry point of the camp, where I would spend my days keeping watch of the goings on from the guard tower. It was high enough that I could also catch a glimpse of what was happening in the second camp, and on more than one occasion I witnessed the stripping of the Jewish prisoners before they were finally led out of sight.

When this happened, they would have to take off all their clothes and jewellery and place them into a very large pile. They would then check their mouths, and some would be chosen and marked. Anyone who dared to make a sound was struck until quiet ensued again. It only took one person as an example, and all the other prisoners would be controllable.

Life inside Treblinka

Not all the prisoners were put on heavy duty, there were some who remained within the camp, and they were given a range of other duties. We had divided the camp into three sections. The first one was where we kept the kitchen and the places for sewing. Then there was the section for those who worked near the train station, and finally, there was the section for those who worked in the sand pit that was massive, and quite close to the camp.

It was quite a distance to walk to the sandpit, and many times while on guard duty, the task seemed incredibly boring. There was an open secret sport that we SS soldiers indulged in whenever we were put on duty to guard the prisoners going to the sand pit. We would shoot for sport, with our targets being the prisoners. As we set out, each of us would choose one that we would shoot for the day. The soldier who managed the quickest death would win. So as they were walking, we would shoot and watch as the chosen prisoner would fall to the ground and die. We would then push their bodies off the path for another soldier to collect and send for cremation.

It gave me some pleasure to see the fear in the eyes of the prisoners, every time that we led the to the sand pit. I felt powerful. Sometimes, just to get them to panic and run, I would cock my gun. The sound alone would have them scatter within seconds so that none of them would be the final target.

There was an ever present smell of flesh from the bodies that were burnt in camp two each day. I hated being near camp two, as there were times the smell was so pungent I could barely take a breath in. Till today, I can barely stand the smell of grilled flesh.

Leaving Treblinka

With soldiers on the way to get us, we had to destroy as much of the camp as was possible. Before we were able to destroy the camp, we had one more thing that needed to be done, and that was to get rid of all the Jews that remained. As German SS soldiers, we knew that the camp was to be liquidated, but the Polish soldiers who were with us, did not know what was to happen. We didn't want to let them know as we had to leave some soldiers behind who would take the fall for all our actions.

Over a short period, we organised the prisoners, leading them into the forest and getting them to dig massive holes there. At the time there were less than 1000 of them left in camp one. Then the day came when we were to dispose of them.

At this time, we had managed to increase the guard with foreign SS soldiers and we began to round up all the prisoners. We made them walk in a single file into the forest, and when we were close to the holes, we started to beat them and subdue them, making them lie down on the ground. Some of us pulled down their trousers so that they would not run. With guns loaded, we started shooting and we did not stop until all of the Jews were lying dead on the ground.

We pushed all their bodies into the ground and covered them up with soil. There was no time to burn them up. We left them there, we left the polish guards there, and we fled to return to Germany.

Till this day, I continue to appreciate the fact that I avoided punishment from the invading forces, as by the time they had arrived at Treblinka, we were long gone. I escaped, though the punishment that I face each day is knowing what had happened to those Jews and the fact that I had turned a blind eye.

Chapter 3:

The Testimony of Maria Berger

My name is Maria Fisch, and I was a soldier in Hitler's army. I was determined to

play my part in the war, and to say the truth, I was a rather headstrong young woman. I got the idea of becoming a part of the army following an advertisement that I saw in the local paper. It was calling for women to join up, to take up easy jobs as guards. Being a woman, I often felt helpless when it came to efforts to help with the war, especially as I did not have any useful skills like sewing or nursing.

I joined the army as an SS-Aufdehrinnen when I was only 24 years old, and I was prepared to face anything, even if it meant that I would be at the front lines. The role of a woman within Hitler's army was still blurry, so I was not sure where I would end up and what I would be given to do. What I did know is that I wanted action and the chance to fight, and I hoped that I would not be given a desk role.

I was given my own service number, 46. Although I had the title of an SS, as a woman it was a challenge to be fully recognised as an SS soldier, although I firmly fell under this jurisdiction. This was the case not only amongst the men who were soldiers, but also amongst other women who had positions in services. For all these groups, I was an anomaly, and they could not understand what was motivating me to go so outside the mould of what was acceptable.

I had another motivation that made me choose to join up, and that was the pay to be received. It was more than I could receive from a normal job, especially as I had not taken the time to develop any particular skills. I believed that every person was aspirational and wanted to earn enough money to secure a comfortable future for themselves and their families. With the money that I would be able to save, I would have a fair start in life, even though I would not be able to get a job. I knew that the war could not last forever, so I needed to capitalise on the opportunity that was before me. It had also been almost impossible to get a regular job, and I was looking for some freedom, away from living with my parents.

I was a guard in the Ravensbruck concentration camp, a camp which had been created for female prisoners, and from the get go, I felt as though I needed to prove myself, especially to prove that I was just as capable of being a soldier as any man. Both the prisoners and the other guards at the camp expected me to be too gentle, and would not speak to me with the respect that I believed I both deserved and had earned. I could not afford to harbour feminine wiles and graces, I had to harden my heart and prove to be tough.

It took a while for me to get acclimatised to the concentration camp, and the way that I needed to behave. I made sure to take some time to watch, especially the way that the other female guards were behaving. They were hard of heart, and cruel, and this was to be my future in the camp. Even though there were things that were happening around, terrible things that would normally have driven me to tears, I could not allow them to dictate the way I would behave and react to situations.

And harden my heart I did. At first I learned how to use my words to inflict verbal abuse, and then I learned how to use my strength for physical abuse. I was renowned for the terror that I inflicted on those around me, especially the women. I had no sympathy for them, whatever condition that they were in. As I started out to prove that I was tougher than any man, I can safely say I did more than accomplish my task. I was terrifying, even to the guards whom I had found at the concentration camp.

When new prisoners arrived at the camp, to keep them in line, I would make sure to give them all a beating at the slightest provocation. All a prisoner needed to do was give me a bad look or clear their throat and I would turn that into a reason to launch a personal physical attack. My reasoning was that when other prisoners say this, they would also fear me, and this would increase the overall respect that I received.

The other male soldiers would laugh and clap every time I hit someone. If anyone proved weak, and showed signs that they could not get the job done, I was merciless, and would send them straight out of the work area, and straight to the chambers where they could be gassed and 'disposed of' in one day. I did not care about human life in this regard, all that I cared about was being sure that I came out on top every time, and that no one could turn around and claim that I had been weak.

As a female guard, I had the privilege of having a dog with me, for purposes of security. Tirelessly, I trained my dog to become a beast that was ruthless, and listed strictly to any command that I would give. For me, the dog was not so much an animal that was meant to tear people limb from limb. The dog was there to behave as my anchor, and to add credibility to everything that I attempted. I used the dog to bring under control those prisoners that were too far for me to reach with my fists. My dog rarely caused any real harm, though she was ideal for causing fear.

This was because as a general rule, I was not permitted to resort to violence on the prisoners without reason (at least not officially), neither was I able to indiscriminately kill any person. That is why I used to draw the line at beatings, as I did not want anyone to die and create problems for me. What I did want was to give them a beating that they would never forget, and this I accomplished several times. I was allowed to give out certain punishments that fit within a certain code. Needless to say, I found numerous opportunities to break the rules. It was not too difficult to do so, as those who were meant to implement the rules were breaking them just as much as I was.

After my first year in the camp, I was able to advance from the position of a guard to that of an overseer. This put me in the position of choosing those who go to the gas chambers and those who are sent for hard labour instead. In addition, I was in charge of the daily roll call which meant that I was also responsible for identifying those who did not have the strength to complete the work, and ensuring they were sent to the gas chambers. Picking off weaklings in the same way as one would pick tomatoes from a vine became second nature to me, and I ensure that everyone who survived the gas chamber was healthy and strong, and able to carry out an extensive work load.

When I joined the army, part of my recruitment qualification was being single and having limited skills. I believe that this was so that I would not be exposed, or have a clear idea of what goes on in the world. I look back at the conditions that I lived in, and why I was happy to stay. I had a pleasant place to live at the camp which allowed me the chance to escape the horrors of each day, and apart from work, the mood at Ravensbruck was usually light-hearted. I almost convinced myself that Germany was not really at war.

Being cruel to women and their children came easily, because I was unable to relate to what it meant to have my own children. It only took me starting my own family to realise the extent of the damage that I caused, and to understand the way that those women must have felt. Now, my heart aches with remorse, and my sleep is plagued with nightmares. It seems to me that I cannot apologise enough, and the ghosts from the past will always haunt me.

Chapter 4:

The Testimony of Alexander Hansen

Hail Hitler!! This is a phrase that is so ingrained in me that I find myself still saying it at the beginning of most of my sentences, especially when I am answering a question or dealing with someone superior. I am Alexander Hansen, former SS soldier. There is so much history that I can share with you, about what it was like becoming a soldier and what led me to that decision, but I would rather tell you about some of the things that I had to do.

When I first joined the army, I was given the position of a driver, and my main responsibility was in the transportation of prisoners. The way that they were transported was important as for the most part, things were to be done below the radar. Even though I did not know what was going to happen to the prisoners at first, letting others know what I was transporting was punishable by death, and so I made sure that the secret was safe with me.

Usually, I was to move them from one camp to another, driving large trucks. Depending on the number of prisoners I would have, some would stand and others would sit. Normally, they would be so many that there was no room for any person to sit down. Everyone would stand up straight for the entire duration of the journey.

Sometimes, I would transport them to the train station, where they would then become the responsibility of another soldier. The trains that they boarded would be heading to a slew of different concentration camps. Although this may sound relatively straightforward, it was a little more sinister as time went on.

The medical field in Germany was growing, and there was an opportunity to become a pioneer in a specific field if one could carry out the right research. As so many of the solutions that were being searched for needed human subjects for testing, the prisoners of war became an excellent resource.

You see, there were always different experiments going on, especially when it came to what to do with prisoners, particularly the Jews. At the time, the directive from Hitler was to eliminate them, and there were camps set up all over Germany and particularly in Poland to do so. As part of the directive, I suddenly had a role to play as a driver.

I was given a new truck to drive, which was designed to keep the Jews in, as well as all the air. Looking at the truck from the outside, it would be impossible to establish who was inside the truck and what was happening as well. The inside of this truck was fully lined with metal, and the floor of the truck was covered with a grill that had been made of wood. There was a pipe connecting to the back of this truck from the exhaust pipe, so that when the motor was on, all the air would fill up the back of the truck. The gas from the running engine was highly toxic, and when inhaled for extended periods of time, would result in instant death that was relatively painless.

On one of my trips, the truck was loaded full of prisoners, and care was taken to ensure that they were all Jews. Therefore, before they were loaded into the truck, a soldier and myself had to do an actual inspection to make sure that only Jews boarded the truck, no matter what country from the region that they came. From. I then started my journey, turning on the motor and slowly driving away. As per my directives, I stopped after a short while, and left the motor running. I waited for fifteen minutes and switched off the ignition. While taking this action, my heart was racing as I was now the one who was tasked with doing the dirty work. I had expected to hear the screams of people dying and there were no screams. I gave it an extra five minutes before determining whether the Jews were alive or dead. When I went to check the back, I found that every single Jew was dead. The experiment had proven to be effective and efficient, attracting minimum attention and ensuring that one can be mobile in a vehicle and still kill the Jews.

After I reported back on the success of this gassing, and confirmed that everyone was dead, I was given a promotion and placed at the Majdanek concentration camp. Although this would have filled the average person with joy, I felt trepidation as I had been so used to the freedom of travel as a driver. I accepted the promotion anyway, and prepared to get to work and do what was expected of me. In the camp I was placed at the gas chambers, so that I could use the Zyklon B gas to exterminate the Jews. I often wondered how I was seen as an expert in this, when I had only managed to complete gassing once, and purely because I was following orders. There was no one whom I could ask why, and get a straight answer from. Therefore, I had to open my mind and be flexible about the advantages of the new position that I was to take up.

Chapter 4: The Testimony of Alexander Hansen

Either way, I had no choice but to accept my new appointment, unless of course I wanted to meet the same fate as those who were to be gassed. When I was not busy controlling the gas that would go into the chambers, I was helping the doctors perfect their experiments. My role was to identify worthy candidates when they came in, ensure that they were Jewish, and then lead them to the doctor. This time, I was in the company of a doctor from the camp who took the time to show me what I was supposed to do. All the Jews were initially lined up inside a room where the doctor would take time to address them while I watched.

The first part of the address was on separation, with women and men being separated. The women who had children were also moved to the side, into a different room. Both the men and women had their heads shaved (as human hair was used to make warm garments) before they were addressed again by the doctor.

The doctor would calmly tell them that they were to have a bath, and the prisoners were all prompted to undress entirely. After this, they were to be led into the supposed bath room, where they believed that they would then be given their new clothing. This room had no windows and two doors. There was the door that they came in through, and the second door which they were supposed to go out of. It was once they were in this room that my job begun.

The room was meant to fill up with as many Jews as possible, in the event that it was necessary to pass them through the gas chamber. The reason being that it took a considerable amount of time to drag out the dead bodies, so it would be much more efficient to ensure that everyone is in the room at the same time.

The room itself was completely airtight, as the only way air could enter the room was through the doors and these sealed tightly when shut and were well bolted down. There was an opening at the gas chamber and it was through this opening that I was to pour the Zyklon B. The opening was high up in the room, so that it would be easier for the gas to permeate and get spread across the entire room. I did this, and was unable to watch what was happening in the room since all the openings were closed. Either way, I do not think that I would have enjoyed watching a live show of the gas and what it does to a human being. However, within minutes, all the Jews had died. I was asked by the doctor to confirm that they were dead, as if the dead silence did not reveal that they were.

There was only one way to make this confirmation in the most accurate way possible, and that was to go and physically check them myself. I would go into the chambers after the gassing and check to see if there was anyone who had a pulse. If they were dead, I was to go through them all to take out gold teeth, and also to remove jewellery that they may have had on, particularly golden rings. This was often quite a challenge, as I had to use a pair of pliers to pull the teeth out. It could be quite troubling at times.

Once I had harvested the bodies of these treasures, they were sent out for cremation where massive furnaces would incinerate them. Sometimes they would be burnt in large pits, and the smoke from their bodies would fill up the sky. The furnaces for cremation were the most preferred as they helped to mask the smell considerably, ensuring that no one was alerted that there was something being burnt on the sight. When cremation had to happen in pits, it would be essential to put all the bodies in the pit as once, so that they get incinerated evenly.

Chapter 4: The Testimony of Alexander Hansen

There was never even one instance when I enjoyed what I had to do, by taking the lives of the prisoners and going through their dead bodies to take away the last of any possessions they may have owned. I had never been a conflict driven person, neither was I out for revenge. When I started out as a driver, I drove the prisoners to their death, but was able to disconnect myself from their fate as I had no direct contact with their exterminations. Once I became an 'expert' at gassing, all this changed. I was relieved when the war came to an end, and was ready to face the consequences for my actions.

I actually hoped that I would be sent to my death, to make up for all the lives that I had personally ended, and this would have been merciful for me. However, my fate was much worse as I was allowed to live, and in life, I cannot erase the memory of what I had done.

Chapter 5:

The Testimony of Reinhardt Kruger

My testimony begins with the words that I lived by from 1942, and which still resonate within my heart to this day – My Honor is named Loyalty. This was what the Fuhrer asked of all the SS soldiers, it was on our official emblem, and it was the standard that I held myself to always. With that in mind, chose to volunteer myself to the cause, by making sure that I found a recruiter.

When I was being recruited, I was glad not to be a part of the Totenkopfverbande as I knew that the real honour would be standing beside our leader as a protector. I was only eighteen when I became an official member of the Waffen-SS, and with my youthful blood boiling in my veins, I was ready to face whatever was going to come my way in the battlefield. I was committed to expressing my loyalty to the Fuhrer at every opportunity that I had.

By the time that I was becoming an SS soldier, things had changed from the way that they were before. I was German and I was Aryan, so believed myself to be above all others. However, there were divisions that had soldiers who were not Aryan, and some of the soldiers were even from different

27

countries. The brutality of the war had changed the dynamics, but at the core of it, we were all fighting on the same side. Like in any war, I had to accept that we had allies, and also that we had our enemies, even though I may not have liked either group very much. Where we used to be the majority, we Germans were now becoming the minority, which would have made my father, had he been alive, shake with anger.

By nature, I was a gentle child, though my burning ambition spurred me forward to do things that I was not always comfortable with. Perhaps I was the wrong person for the army, but the chance to prove myself to be a man was too much for me to simply rest and do something else. I knew about war, that I would have to kill people in order to protect my country. I understood that these people were dangerous and would kill me if I did not kill them. What I did not understand were the horrors that came with these acts. Having the power to take a life does not mean that you should take one. The moment that you kill a person, something deep inside you will change for all time.

Anyway, I became a member of the 6th SS Kampfgruppe Nord, when the unit was being rebuilt following the battle of 1941 which had taken place in northern Russia and Finland. Following this battle, there were many lives that had been lost and I believed that I was just part of the team that were meant to replace these soldiers. After all, the front could not be left bare and open to threats from all the surrounding.

I saw a different side to the war, because of where my division and I were stationed. We were at the Kestenga front, and following the Soviet offensive that had occurred the year before, there was not much action in our area. I spent my days in the trenches, waiting for something to happen, looking up at the sun and sky, playing games with my comrades, and feeling as though I was not serving any purpose. All this was done at heightened alert, so I found that my body was always tensed up and I experienced more and more episodes of pain and feelings of discomfort.

I was not alone in this feeling, as many of the people who were with me were also affected. Boredom did not bode well with us. At any opportunity we got, we would defend ourselves aggressively, using even the most minute attack as an outlet to elevate our daily activities. It was from this boredom that I made a terrible mistake that would change my experience of the war completely.

The problem began when I got into an argument with my fellow comrade, Hans Dietrich about what it meant to be a true German. I was feeling entitled, frustrated from the boredom, and annoyed that anyone would dare to object with my point of view. What had started out as a simple exchange of words soon escalated and we were amidst a rage fuelled physical fight. It was then that I reached for my rifle, and shot Hans in the middle of his chest. Other comrades had by then arrived to separate us, but they stood stunned in silence as we watched his body flop over.

I was speechless. I had come to fight my enemy, and yet in my blind rage, had killed a friend instead, and over something that was not even important. As an SS soldier, I had shown that I was not worthy, having shot a man who was unarmed. It was not long before I was taken out of the trenches and given a quick judgement from the SS courts. I was to be sent to the Dachau camp, where I would become a prisoner of war.

The journey to Dachau began, and I was in such distress that I did not notice how long it took, or the sights and places that we passed along the way. Shame was eating away at me. Guilt as well for my thoughtless action. Fear and uncertainty about the future were at the foremost of all my thoughts. I was worried about going against my honor, and determined to prove that this action would never change my loyalty. When I arrived at Dachau, I was taken up to the prison which was on the east side of the camp. There I found another 117 soldiers, who had all committed one criminal act or another. Compared to the rest of the prisoners in the camp, we were a small number. I was grateful that we have been put together, and remained protected as a unit.

We were all subject to the jeers and insults of our guards, all of whom were foreigners that had become SS soldiers. It was beyond humiliating, and sometimes, I prayed fervently for death to come upon me. Slowly, my body began to become weaker and weaker due to the lack of nutrition that I had once become accustomed to, and I barely had enough energy to complete the tasks that were on assignment to me each day.

One day, I will never forget the day, the 29th of April in 1945, all of us incarcerated SS soldiers were called and put into a line. The foreign soldiers were leaving, and it was impossible to find out why since they would never address us directly, unless it was to put us in line with the butt of a gun. They refused to share the reason, choosing instead to give us weapons. We were ordered to take control of the camp and guard all of the prisoners.

I knew that there was something amiss, but the urge to hold a gun in my hands again left me without any questions. Once again, I was to hold a position of honour instead of shame, and I was ready for that. My other comrades were very wary of this new show of kindness, feeling that it may be a trap or some new way of punishment that had a terrible end.

Before we went out to see what was happening with the other prisoners, we sat together for a little while and discussed what we should do. Checking the weapons we had been given, we realised that they had real ammunition, and that we were truly armed. With confidence that we could defend ourselves, we made our way into the rest of the camp.

Before us, there were a considerable number of prisoners, all huddled together in little groups with questions in their eyes. We were in the process of guarding them by rounding them all up in the best way that we could when the entire camp was stormed by soldiers.

Upon close examination, it became clear that the new soldiers were not German at all, neither were they SS soldiers from any of the other countries that were fighting with the Germans. They were actually Americans, and they had come to liberate the prisoners. It was then that I understood why I had been given the weapon and the directive to guard the prisoners. It was the final betrayal that we would face, as we were now in the hands of the enemy, and appeared to be the cause of the problems that were facing the prisoners at that time. Although the situation was unfair, I felt as though I had deserved it as a punishment for what I had done to Hans.

I was put on trial by the Americans, and they were keen to prove that I was amongst those who abused the prisoners, and that I, as well as the other 'guards' that they found were killing people who had been held prisoner indiscriminately. Through the entire trial period, it was unearthed that those of us who had been captured were indeed SS soldiers, and had been at the Dachau camp as prisoners for various crimes. Finding little testimony to support the claims that had been made against us, even after a thorough investigation had been carried out, we were free to go.

Chapter 5: The Testimony of Reinhardt Kruger

I realised that I could never return to my home again, as I would be viewed as someone who had betrayed the position that I had been given. Even though I knew that I had done no such thing, I had faced enough large groups to anticipate the negative reaction that I would have been subject to receiving. I wanted to be free to live my life, though it may have been better if I had died. Instead, I made the decision to find the next ship out of Germany and head to America, where I could start an entirely new life.

This is exactly what I did. I remember taking my first deep breath of American air. Things were going to be better for me. I believed it. Even so, my life in Germany, my home, the thoughts of my German friends were never too far away from me.

So my testimony is about survival, and near misses. I missed great battles, and the only time I did shoot someone, it was a fellow SS soldier. I spent time in prison, and was set up for false accusations by the American soldiers. Even with all this, and many other atrocious experiences, I survived to tell the tale. Some think that I should not have done so – but I am here anyway. Whatever anyone thinks, I still believe to this day that My Honor is named Loyalty.

Chapter 6:

The Testimony of Rudolf Schreiber

It was 1942, and I was fed up with the war. It is not that I did not understand the reason that we were at war, I was simply frustrated at the lack of information on what was really happening, as it was clear that something was happening. I wanted to get to the bottom of everything, to what could be called the real story. I needed to know more than the propaganda that was being fed to citizens, many of whom were going on with their daily lives as though the war was a fender bender, rather than a head on collision.

I was working as a journalist, and not a very successful one at that. It is not that I lacked the stories to tell, it was the fact that only a few papers wanted to publish my work. I had earned a reputation for being cut-throat and honest.

I was German, living in Germany and working in Germany. There had been whispers about the deaths of Jews, and special camps of death where they were being killed. As much as I tried to dig around to find out the real story, I never could as the whispers would be subdued with incredible speed. I tried questioning former army officials, soldiers who were fighting in the army, as well as the SS soldiers who were fighting for

Hitler's army. No matter which avenue or angle that I attempted to follow, I was consistently turning up empty.

So I decided the best thing to do was to go undercover, and find out for myself what was really happening. At 22 years old, I was young enough, strong enough and sufficiently ignorant to join the war efforts as a soldier. So I applied to become a member of the SS and before I could even take a breath, I had been admitted into one of the divisions. This was exciting as I'd expected the process would be much longer and time consuming. I found that I was encouraged and then motivated.

Initially, I was placed in administration, and tasked with sourcing and sorting the supplies that went to the camp. I spent what seemed like an eternity confirming stocks of sardines, ham and water for the other soldiers. Even though the work proved to be quite tedious, I did it all myself and gave my very best. After a while, I was appointed with delivering these supplies and it is at this time that my choice to join the SS and do something physically active in the field became worthwhile.

In one of my deliveries, I was tasked with delivering Prussic Acid to one of the camps, I forget which one now. I had never heard of this acid, and I could not understand what it could be for. I wondered whether I had made a mistake, but when I reached the camp, it was one of the expected items. I asked there what this was for, and I was simply told 'gas chamber.'

I was stunned to find that there was some truth to the rumours. I wanted to know more and became friends with one of the SS guards at a camp I delivered to often, the Auschwitz camp. In our conversations, I learnt that the Jews would be sent to rooms, where they would be stripped naked, and within minutes, they would be gassed and killed. After that, all evidence would need to be destroyed, and the bodies of the Jews would be quickly cremated, or they will be buried in mass graves.

The horror that was described to me was so real, it was almost palpable, and I found that I faced a real challenge putting down what I had heard into words. I found it hard to believe, and wanted to witness it for myself. I had a responsibility to share with my readers what was happening around them, and therefore, I could not dismiss the truth. It needed to come out.

I asked for a transfer, from administration to a concentration camp, and to my surprise, it was granted. The main reason that I was surprised was how easy it was, no questions asked. I was taken to a camp at Belzec, and put on duty as a guard. I knew that in this position, I would be able to find out a lot about the goings on at the camp.

I saw first-hand, thousands of Jews being led to their deaths. They would arrive at the camp, go through a sorting process, and the large number would end up in the gassing room. Before they are led into the room, they are asked to undress and strip down to nothing. The next step is for them to be led into the bedroom. In this room, the Prussic Acid would be poured in, and within minutes, the Jews and any other prisoners with them would be dead.

At the time I wanted to send an anonymous story to as many governments as I could to let the world know about what was happening. I hoped that if I did this, then there would be some sort of cavalry, and help would come to save the prisoners. I was German, and wanted to be German, but not at the cost of innocent lives, even the lives of children.

Chapter 6: The Testimony of Rudolf Schreiber

What stopped me from pushing forward with my plan was the actions that the Fuehrer would take against me. At the camp that I was in, the prisoners were not only Jews and foreign nationals. There were also Germans in the camp, some who were political prisoners, and others who were suspected of treason. All of them were destined to have the same experience. I would ask myself, what good am I to the world if I am dead and cannot tell my story?

It was less than three months before all of the atrocities came to an end, and the French arrived to take over the camp. I was arrested as an SS soldier, and turned into one of the prisoners that I used to guard. I watched them all go free, and wondered what was to be my fate. When the time for my trial arrived, I explained my intentions, the reason I joined the army, what I had done as a soldier, and what I believed Germany stood for. I simply spoke my truth, expressing my disappointment in my country, and the way that the prisoners were treated. It was an excellent and true tail, but the judge found it challenging to believe fully.

I was sentenced to prison, and since I had not murdered anyone by my own hand, I only needed to stay a prisoner for five years. In that time, I managed to write down my story, the one that I hoped would build my career.

I never did get the story published in the end, as I had not anticipated that my experience as a soldier would change me as a person. I never anticipated that I would experience intense guilt for the role that I had chosen to play and the sadness and despair that resulted because of my ambition.

My testimony is that I stood by and watched, due to being too afraid to make any real changes. I did not become a cruel soldier, like so many that I encountered, but I did not make any attempt to change things while I was a soldier. That is the guilt that I carry around me which I expect to remain until my dying day.

Chapter 7:

The Testimony of Franz Rietscher

I was born in Finland, and my parents named me Abel, with my surname being Ferencz. The Second World War started when I was just 17 years old, and before my very eyes, the people that I had known and grown up with began to disappear and move away, as the Germans gained power. By the time I was 19, I was faced with an interesting ultimatum, to join the German forces or risk death.

I chose to join the forces and thus started to serve in the Waffen SS. I knew that I had what it takes to join the normal army, but I needed to challenge myself and prove that I could do better. This is why I chose to join Hitler's army. The Germans had begun to look beyond their borders to build on the army, and there were small legions coming up in several countries of non-German SS soldiers. As a soldier, I was expected to go into the battle field, and fight for Germany at the front.

It was when I became an SS soldier that I decided to change my name to the more German Franz Rietscher. I did this so that I could be better identified with Germany, and also because I did not want to stand out as being different from all the other soldiers. As it was, the Germans had believed that they were the superior race, and I did not want to have it discovered that I did not belong to that category.

It is not that I wanted to help the Germans in any way, it is more that we had the same enemy. That was the soldiers from the Soviet Union. While the Germans were busy taking over territories all around my country, the Soviets had invaded us and were leading us with a heavy hand of terror. They were pushing their ideals for communism at every country that they encountered, and this was not the direction that German's wanted to go in. We were determined not to accept the situation by simple surrender. We were ready to fight.

By joining the SS, I believed that I was doing what I could to be patriotic and protect my people, especially those who had become prisoners of war. I learnt to speak German, and even was able to mask my accent quite well. I was intent on not revealing my true identity, in case this led to my being victimised or even killed.

Sure enough, as expected I was sent to the front, where I fought alongside German soldiers. I did what I could, and after four months, I was elevated and moved up the ranks. By this time, my cover was beginning to wear a little thin, as there were questions that I could not adequately answer about being German. However, there was nothing that the German soldiers could do about it. Because of my rank, they were forced to salute me and follow my orders.

Although I was not Jewish, I had family members who were, and I was stricken by what was happening to the Jews. I was not the only Finnish man to risk becoming an SS soldier, and I had other comrades in arms from my country, some of whom were Jews, yet fighting for the same cause that I was. It was safer for us to be a part of the SS army than in any other army or position, as this would save us the experiences of cruelty as prisoners, or of being separated from family and so on.

It was impossible to deny one's true self for so long, and the Germans who fought alongside us figured it out soon enough. No matter how hard I tried, there were some mannerisms and cultural nuances that had been with me since birth, and it was challenging trying to change them to fit into the situation I was in. Most of the time, any mistakes that I made were from being conscious of what is needed.

Many of them would express their shock, not because of the fact that they were fighting with Jews, against Jews, but because the Jews were just as human as they were. Many believed that Jews were like animals, and were not really human. Fighting with them gave them new insight, and I am sure we led some of our comrades to question their own beliefs. This was not by their own fault, but rather, based on the system of education that they were growing up with, as well as the influence from their older peers who would let them know that there was a problem with Jews.

I was not kept at the front line for very long after my promotion. They needed foreign soldiers in one of the camps, to help control the prisoners of war who were there. It was around 1944 by then, and it seemed as though the Germans were slowly mobbing back into Germany, and leaving the camps that were outside Germany under the power of other soldiers.

I found myself in Germany, where I was sent to a camp called Dachau. It was one of the oldest concentration camps at the time, and it held a range of prisoners, mainly Germans who had committed political crimes, and foreign nationals who had the misfortune of being in Germany at the wrong time, having been perceived of taking the wrong actions.

I was sent to the medical building in the camp, where my duties included controlling the prisoners as they awaited different medical tests, taking them back to their section in the camp once the tests were completed, and then on occasion, taking bodies to the disposal site when they did not survive the tests.

The tests that the prisoners were going through were not the normal medical tests that check for levels of blood pressure and so on. These were highly invasive tests, many of which even required the prisoner being cut open so that something could be observed. All sorts of horrific things happened to the prisoners. One would think that the weakest would be picked for the tests, but it was actually the stronger prisoners that I witnessed being taken for tests. The Germans were terrified of catching any illnesses, so when the prisoners were being infected with different diseases to see how they would cope with them, it was foreign soldiers such as myself who would be left to interact with the prisoners.

The testing was relentless, and if a prisoner did not die, then they would be tested on over and over again. If they became too weak, they would be sent off to another camp, where I believe they would be killed. They were simple subjects, and were treated in the same way that one would treat a rat within a laboratory. As though they were voiceless, thoughtless and devoid of all feelings. There were prisoners who suffered throughout the war due to hard labour and beatings, but they were able to recover from these. Those prisoners who were exposed to the medical testing and experiments rarely recovered, and many were left with internal and external scars that lasted a lifetime.

The day of liberation finally came, a day that I will never forget. It was the 29th of April, in 1945. The day started out as normal, though there was some tension in the air. Following the death of Hitler, things had been slightly unbalanced although it was not too severe. As it moved forward, what seemed like hordes of other foreign soldiers descended upon the camp. Most of them were American. They were eliminating the German SS soldiers who tried to create a defence around the camp.

I remember throwing down my weapon, and for the first time in years, I identified myself with my real name. I was trying my best to speak in what had once been my natural accent as I did not want to be identified as a German. I do not think they understood what I was really saying, but having my hands in the air and in effect surrendering helped to save me.

More than 30,000 prisoners were saved that day, although many did not live much longer after the liberation. They had been through too much to pick up their lives again. I was glad that my life was spared, even though I was a soldier. I was glad that I fought for my country.

Chapter 8:

The Testimony of Ulrich Schafer

The war had been raging for months, and each day seemed to get worse for me. Let me introduce myself. I am Ulrich Schafer and at the time that the war was coming to a close, I was turning 22 years old. How I had managed to survive all the atrocities that I had seen remains a mystery to me until today. Although joining the army at the age of 20, I was considered old, I still chose to do so.

It took me longer than most of my age mates to join in the war efforts, as I was the first born of five children, and my father had lost his life fighting for what he believed in as a soldier. My mother in devastation became catatonic, and was unresponsive to almost all things. It was up to me to hold the family together, and I did so for as long as I could. When my sister turned 18 years old, I felt it prudent for me to do my part for the country, and with that I volunteered to became an SS soldier.

As an SS soldier, I would receive much more respect that a normal soldier. This is because although I was part of an army, I was not in the army. The SS included soldiers who descended from the body guards of Adolf Hitler, a highly coveted position indeed.

Chapter 8: The Testimony of Ulrich Schafer

Upon being recruited, I went through vigorous preparation and training, as only the strongest would survive and hold on to their position. I was amongst the strongest, and following my training was to be sent to the frontline. However, due to some agreement that was made with the General I reported to, I was sent to do guard duty at the Treblinka camp. The reason that my general gave was that I was too old to go to the front, they preferred to sacrifice those that were much younger than myself.

When I think about the Treblinka camp, I hate to think about or even speak about the things that I did and the things that I saw. No human should have to carry with them those burdens, although without choice I carry these burdens with me every day. Stories of atrocities are fascinating to hear, but gruelling to tell. My testimony is all about what happened when the war was over – when we were forced to surrender.

There was chatter everywhere about the war coming to an end as the Fuhrer had taken his own life. Words cannot describe the worry and anxiety that us soldiers experienced after this event. Adolf Hitler had been our charismatic leader, the one whom we all believed in and were fiercely loyal to. Without him, it was hard to imagine an anchor that could keep us granted, or even picture anyone who had the same energy to take his place.

We had been ordered by the generals to leave our camps, and we were lost, with a fear of the unknown and what was going to happen to us. Rumour had it that there were invasions happening all around the country, and that our enemy forces were infiltrating our camps and taking over. The only way that we would be able to save ourselves is if we abandoned all the prisoners and quite literally, ran for our lives.

It was the 8th of May in 1945 when Germany chose to surrender to the allies, marking the end of the war. That night, for the first time, my future seemed so uncertain, as what I had been fighting for and what I believed in appeared to be coming to nought. When I sought council from my comrades, it became apparent that we all had the same feelings, thoughts and doubts. The unknown was daunting, and we were unsure of how much longer we would be in hiding. We noticed that most of the invaders were American troops, and they seemed to be everywhere at once.

We had surrendered as Germans, but I still had plenty of fight within me. As far as I was concerned, I personally had not surrendered, even though I had been ordered to do so. I took my ultimate orders from Adolf Hitler, and without him being alive, I was willing to risk going rogue. In a heated discussion with my comrades it was agreed that we would not be taken without a fight, that we would rather go down dying than simply give in to the enemy. Despite our bravado, when the soldiers from the US descended upon us, we found that our ammunition was not enough for even the most paltry defence. Without any choice, we gave ourselves up.

They were rounding up all the German soldiers, and freeing all the prisoners of war – the people whom we had held captive for betraying us and going against our values. I had always looked upon them with disdain, yet seeing them at that point, staggering around in emaciated confusion, I felt what I can only describe as a twinge of remorse, though it was the slightest twinge. The feeling soon disappeared. I had been angry and ready to fight for so long that there was no room within me for tender feelings.

Chapter 8: The Testimony of Ulrich Schafer

I wanted to speak to my fellow comrades, but the words could not come out. I was completely trapped in my thoughts, thinking up elaborate escape plans, figuring out how I was going to survive this situation, planning how I could overcome one of the US soldiers, being plagued by constant thoughts. With this mind set, I walked aimlessly, following the crowd to where we were being led, walking in silence. I noticed that all the prisoners were watching from the side lines, and this time, it was the turn of the guards to experience the ultimate humiliation.

I found that myself in a large field, with what seemed like thousands of my comrades. Our weapons and other items had previously been confiscated, so all I had on me were the clothes on my back and the will in my heart. We simply stood there and waited. We would stand, sit, lie down, try and move around, but never once did we attempt to escape our fate. We were too proud to be regarded as cowards, and would have faced any punishment head on. Days and nights came and went and we continued to remain in the field, with minimal room for movement, no tents to protect our heads and bodies from the elements, and nothing that we could eat.

Things went from bad to worse, and it reached a point where I saw people consuming their own faeces – they had long been drinking their own urine anyway. The US soldiers were a force that always patrolled around us, watching us and being menacing enough for no one to believe that they would survive an attempt at escape, and indeed no one bothered to try. When these soldiers got bored, they would find a way to amuse themselves, and this normally entailed them taking one of us out from the crowd and practicing their shooting skills.

Although this may have seemed cruel, I found that I was not moved or angered by their actions. Being a soldier myself I had done the very same things, and I was actually grateful. Had they done to us what we would have done to them if they were our prisoners, death would have been all too welcome.

Finally, a meal!

It seemed like it had been months, but only a week had passed since my last meal. I felt as though my body had become accustomed to living without nourishment. I knew that if I began to think about the situation with food, I would die before the end of the day. Everything was getting bleaker and bleaker, and I was sure that my life was coming to an end soon. I took pride in the fact that even though I was destined to die, I would not die as a coward.

It was then that I noticed the aircraft that was bringing us food provisions, and I believe that is the first time I can say my heart skipped a beat. For me, that plane was like a long lost love, coming to remind me that they still care. The plan had lowered itself as close to the ground as possible, and then dropped a large package that was to contain the food all were yearning for.

Instead of finding food that we could eat, all that had been placed within the package was butter. Some of the men who were ravenous ate the butter without abandon, though I took a moment before I started eating. I wondered why they would bring plain butter, but the hunger I was experiencing was too much for me to reason logically. I needed to put something inside my stomach, and so I did.

Chapter 8: The Testimony of Ulrich Schafer

Before long, there were some people with upset stomachs, some of whom actually died. It was too much for them to ingest the butter after weeks of not eating properly, and rather than giving lasting sustenance, the butter caused pain, and quite possibly clogged some of the veins.

The following day, the sound of the plane could be heard overhead again, and as it drew nearer, it become clear that it was also carrying a package. This plane then dropped some bread, which I assumed was supposed to go with the butter. This time I ate slowly so as not to upset my stomach, and the bread tasted like the best food I had ever eaten.

Through keeping a keen ear on the ground, I heard that the food had always been available, but the soldiers from the US did not believe that we were ready for it. In their own cruel way, they hid all the food, watching us starve and suffer. Apparently, the US soldiers found this fun. I think that those who had not faced the horrors of being in the frontline at the battlefield were facing prisoners for the first time, and that they enjoyed the power which was being wielded onto them.

Before long, we were all tried for our crimes and imprisoned, and now, I am out of prison and living my life as a free man. I sometimes chuckle to myself at the attempt the Americans made at cruelty. This is not a chuckle of amusement, more one of wonderment. Yes, there are those who died from their antics, but had we been given the chance to punish the American soldiers in one of our camps, we would have been much more cruel and effective.

Chapter 9:

The Testimony of Kurt Schmidt

My name is Kurt Schmidt and I was a guard who was stationed at Treblinka for a few months before the war came to an end. For decades I have had a heavy heart, finding it impossible to share what I had experienced. Now, I share these experiences with you as I approach my last days. I do not want to reach the gates of heaven with them inside me. Yes, I was an SS soldier and have forgiven myself for all the things that I did. Heaven is my destiny.

During the war, I loved the role that I had to play. What drew me to this role the most was the power that I wielded. People would see me in my uniform and immediately cower in fear. They would speak to me with carefully selected words, and almost always, looked down so that they would not have to look at me in the eye. This power was like a drug, which was fuelled by my other SS comrades and the man that I looked up to above all others, Adolf Hitler himself.

I was only 18 years old in those final months of the war, and deeply believed that I had fought the good fight, a belief I still hold to this day. I know that if man does not have something that drives action, then there is nothing to really live for.

Chapter 9: The Testimony of Kurt Schmidt

Back to my testimony. The inmates in Treblinka clearly outnumbered the guards, and should there have been any type of uprising, the war would have been over much earlier. However, everyone was scared, especially the prisoners, and they followed instructions without question, until it was too late for them to turn back.

Treblinka was divided into two sections, what I like to call the upper camp and the lower camp. My position was in the upper camp, which was decidedly gruesome as it was in this section of the camp that one could find the gas chambers. Within these chambers, we eliminated the Jews and other prisoners who had proven themselves to be a threat to the Germans.

One thing that many people do not take into account is the issue of responsibility, or maybe I could better describe this with one of the modern terms of today, 'getting the hands dirty'. There was a job that needed to be done, and truth be told, the nature of the job was not pleasant. In my case, the job was to lead people through the upper camp and into one of the six large gas chambers. There, the doors would be shut so that the room was airtight, and then the gassing would begin.

Under my command were foreign soldiers, who I delegated the most unpleasant tasks to. They had the role of directing all the prisoners of war into the gas chamber, in the most quietly and orderly way possible. For most of the prisoners, the gas chambers were a simple rumour which they could not substantiate, as others who had arrived before them had not survived to tell a tale.

The prisoners would be kept in order, often believing that they were walking towards their final cells, to wait out their sentences and hope to survive. Hope had no place in the war. I would make sure that there were as many people in the gas chambers as possible, so that the task of gassing them would be over faster, and we could then move on to the next batch.

If a gas chamber could fit 300 people within it, I would try to push the envelope and have 350 people packed into the chamber. I would give myself a target of prisoners that would be gassed in day, and had a personal sense of pride when I surpassed my own target.

Once in the gas chamber, screams of confusion could be heard, as the prisoners began to panic realising that they were in a windowless room and had been shut in. Then the gassing would begin.

As was the fashion at the time, I tried to ensure that I never actually moved the lever to release the gas into the chamber myself. I would find someone to delegate this task to. Within a few short minutes, the once loud screams would become whimpers, and this would then be followed by silence. When there was no sound to be heard, the release of the gas would be halted, and after a few minutes, the foreign guards would go into the chambers to ensure all had perished. They would then drag the bodies out so that we could prepare for their disposal.

When I look back at my life at that time, I feel sorry for those who died, and for the families that were destroyed as a result of the deaths within the gas chambers. However, I have no remorse over what I did.

This may seem to be cold, though I realised a long time ago that even if I had the chance to turn the hands of time back, my actions would not vary. I believe that since I did not actively kill anyone, that my participation was passive and instructional, I am absolved of the guilt that the foreign soldiers who led people into the chambers are facing. I believe that at that age, all that I really knew was what had been told to me. I belonged to a movement of people who had a strong belief, and lived by their ideals.

My testimony is not an apology, and this should not lead anyone to judge my actions. I had a concern that others would never understand, and would perceive me as being cold or unfeeling. This is far from the case. I have a clear conscience because I never got my hands dirty.

Chapter 10:

The Testimony of Gunther Kramer

My testimony begins towards the end of 1944, when I was given the unlikely chance to join the army. Unlikely because I was only 15 years old, and all that I could remember about my time growing up was fighting, bombs going off and hatred. In my household, my parents always seemed to be on edge, and if they were not shouting at one another, they were sitting staring into different directions in silence. In fact, this was normal for all my friends as well, and very much accepted as the way of life.

I was skilled at listening out for bombs or explosions, and rallying my younger sister and brother together so that we could get cover until the sound was gone. I knew that the war meant that people would die, and I had already began realising that all the older boys had disappeared. They would show up one day in bright new uniforms, and looked so smart. I knew that people would be proud of them and look happy when waving them away, but after they would leave, their mothers would start crying. I thought it was strange.

One day a message was making the rounds in the town where I lived, and the news was there had been a campaign and Normandy, and too many young lives had been lost. I thought about all the friends I had who had gone to fight, but since no one mentioned any of them by name, I assumed that they were safe. It was then that I was stopped by a man dressed in SS uniform, who told me that he was a recruiter for the army. I told him I was 15 years old, and he asked me whether I wanted to be a man, and if I was proud of being German. I puffed up my chest and agreed fervently. He congratulated me and told me that I was not in Hitler's army. It was then that I rushed home to tell my mother and father the 'good' news.

Their reactions were as I had assumed they would be. Having watched all those people going away, I knew that there would be a mix of happiness and sadness. Upon hearing the news, they were crestfallen, with my mother in a stunned silence and a glazed look in her eye, and my father patting me on the back as if to congratulate me, yet holding on to my shoulders as if he did not want me to leave. I pictured myself looking like a soldier and marching up and down, and was thrilled to have the chance to do so.

I expected to be taken for training, as my father had told me. First, we would be trained to become stronger and withstand the elements, and then we would learn the different drills and how to march. He said that this would be followed by being able to shoot a gun to protect ourselves, and once we are finally ready, we will be able to go to war. On the day that I waved goodbye to my parents and siblings, I was not afraid that I would die. I worried about whether I could survive the training, and how quickly I could move up the ranks and become a general! I had glory in my eyes.

We were a group of boys from my village that arrived at the training camp, and the first night, we were allowed to sleep early. Following the separation from our families, it was expected that we would be sad and need some time to readjust, even if it was just for a few hours. For me, there was no misery or sadness, only anticipation for what was coming in the future. I was now a part of the Hitlerjugend. In the morning, amidst shrill whistles and yells we were woken up. Having never been awoken like this before, I was in total shock. I was sluggish for a moment as I tried to figure out where I was, but once I did, I jumped up and dressed with haste. The day was going to be bright as I got to do what soldiers do.

Our first stop was the training field, and here, I held my very first gun. Things were not happening as my father had told me, but I did not care. I was in the army now. We were told that we had to learn how to survive a gun fight, and that we should always always kill the enemy. I learnt how to shoot a gun that very first day, and in the week that followed, was intensively trained on how to put together and maintain my weapon, how to hide so that I could not be seen, when would be the right time to shoot, and various other tactics that governed my survival skills. I also learned how to fight with my bare hands and with small weapons. I felt that I was on top of the world, and was confident enough to believe that no enemy could overcome my attacks. Little did I realise that I would soon be at the front lines, with only my newly learned skills to keep me going.

The older generals who were training us young recruits always found fault in what we were doing. This is because we were willing to shoot the enemy, but we were not bloodthirsty. Instead, we were excited, as indeed we were school boys and life had just taken an interesting turn, becoming a real adventure. Everything was new to us, and we did not understand what it meant to take the life of another person. We would only play pretend, laughing over ourselves when it was someone's turn to act out that they keep over and die.

One thing that I noticed was that there were no men who were in their twenties. Most of the boys who were there were around my age, and the people who were training us were all so much older, in that they had white hairs. Everyone seemed to be much older than they actually were as I found out that some of the white haired men were only in their thirties. In my naïveté, I believed that every one of the young men must all be out fighting at the front lines. They must have been thrilled. The day came when my comrades and I were informed that we were going to see the enemy face to face. The battles were becoming more vicious by the day, and our training was veering towards the fanatical. We were to be sent to the trenches.

We spent two days travelling to the trenches, and when we arrived, all seemed to be quiet as there was no shooting happening around us. We were told that we would need to spend at least three days in the trenches before anyone would come to look for us. The simple instruction that we were given was that if anyone started shooting at us, we were to shoot right back. It sounded simple enough. We talked in whispers as the sun set and waited for time to get some sleep.

When the darkness seemed to be at its thickest, almost like a blanket, there was a whistling sound and before we knew what was happening, there were explosions everywhere. I watched as all around me, my comrades were falling having been hit by grenades or gunshots. They seemed to be coming from everywhere, and even though I had been told to shoot, I had no idea where I was going to shoot. I was frozen.

Something hit me in the head and the darkness seemed to envelope me as I fell. I was sure that I had died. However, at some point, I came too, opening my eyes as the heat of the sun seemed to burn into my skin. My head hurt more than it had ever done before, and when I opened my eyes to look around me all that I saw were dead bodies.

So this was the reality of war. I tried to crawl around and see if anyone else would wake up, but nobody did. That afternoon, the general sent someone to check for survivors and I was found. I was the only one who made it out alive, and I was shaken beyond all belief.

After a while in the infirmary, where it was found that a bullet had grazed the side of my head, I was sent back home to my family. Within two days I celebrated my 16th birthday. I have never been able to get the pictures of the dead out of my head, and have never truly recovered from my time in battle.

I sometimes wonder why I was the only one who survived, and then I stop. There is no point to wonder as there is no clear answer. My testimony is that I lived, and God himself knows why he spared me.

Chapter 11:

The Testimony of Hans Braun

I come from a proud Aryan family, with a mother and father who constantly reminded me that I should hold my head up high for being a pure German, without blemish and authentically Aryan. We were the greatest race that had ever lived.

In 1935, I was only 16, living in Germany, and wanting to make a name for myself. My father was a captain in the German army, having served the country during the first world war. When I looked upon him, I saw a brave man who could do no wrong, and more than anything, I wanted him to be proud of me. As time moved forward, I realised that there was one thing that I could achieve that would make him proud. That was becoming one of the SS soldiers, the elite individuals that were tasked with providing security to our patron, Adolf Hitler.

I was drafted as an SS soldier in 1940, just after I had turned 21 years old. I was not expected to immediately go out into the field and do battle. Instead, I was not recommended for field work at all. As I had some experience handling logistics, I was put in charge of taking care of meals to the prisoners who were in the front line. For this to happen, I needed to be able to coordinate an armoured track, and have on-ground contacts who would help to retrieve and distribute what was available. It was during this time that I saw the war, live and in action.

The trenches were not permanently fixed in their sides and depth, they were continuously being built up so that they would become longer and reach further areas for better coverage and defence. When making food deliveries, it was essential to know this so that the food could be delivered to the right section with ease.

I had been stationed close to the border of Poland, and sent to the trenches in the rainy season. Being close to a border meant that I needed to be extra vigilant, and the cold water as rain also affected my overall comfort. I had not been taught about how to best protect my feet so after a short while, I suffered from frost bite and three toes.

After I had recovered fully, I was given lighter duties within the camp, including the management of all the laundry and helping to ensure that all the soldiers have everything that the need, clearly labelled, before they head out into the battle field.

For the longest time, I felt as though I had been demoted, and not given the position that I deserved. I did not realise that the position I was in was amongst the best that one could have in the war. The frontlines were highly dangerous, as a person could get shot in an instant. In my position, I had minimal enemies, as during an attack, little attention is paid to those who are offering support.

Where at first I took umbrage at being bypassed and kept away from the frontline, I can to realise that I was far more important that a gun for hire. I was the brave one who ensured that the army had the energy that they needed to fight. Today, I keep away from trenches, and make sure that my feet are always well wrapped. I have the constant reminder of three missing toes, which ensure that all bases are checked before I approach anyone or anything.

Conclusion

One thing that comes out clearly from the testimonies in this book is that SS soldiers were not all the same. There are those who imagined that they were all cruel and ruthless, and that they simply walked around shooting people at will. However, the stories of the SS soldiers were much deeper than that. They help you to see into the heart of the soldiers, and walk through the journeys that they needed to follow to get to their own liberation.

These testimonies reveal the role of the forgotten, including those soldiers who were female, those from other countries, and those who were so young that they did not fully comprehend what it meant to be a soldier, and what they were expected to do. They are not all accounts of regrets, and some are just memories, taking you through the steps and issues that were encountered.

All in all, these testimonies put you in the heart of the war, and tell tales that connect you with the feelings of those who were a part of the war. It is important to live these tales, in the same way as those who told them. It gives those who lost their lives some respect, as greater understanding is accorded to their situation.

None of the SS soldiers that survived had a happy life afterwards. They were haunted by what they had seen, and by the acts that they had committed. The testimonies of here are

Conclusion

from the lucky ones, those who did not receive the punishment of death for their crimes. Keep these people in your thoughts, and open up your hearts to forgive.

The Holocaust

------ ❧❦❧ ------

The Story of a Jewish Survivor

Introduction

The course of my life has been an interesting one, coloured by experiences that would cripple the functioning of the typical person. However, these experiences have been a source of strength for me. I lived. I survived. And this is my story.

Many years ago, I lived in Poland, in the town of my birth Krakow. I had a loving family, and a fantastic life. I was a beautiful young lady, looking to the future with hope and joy. All that changed in the blink of an eye, when the realities of the Holocaust became my daily reality. I watched around me as people were murdered or died from terrible conditions, all in a bid to get rid of all Jewish people.

How I survived all those years remains a mystery to me, and when I look back at my life, I realise that I experienced one miracle after another. I have decided to share these experiences as best I can with you, and hope that you will see in them the miracles that have kept me alive.

Although my experiences are painful, and I endured more than what most people should, I survived. I now feel I have a responsibility to be the voice for all those who did not get the chance to have a voice, who died during the Holocaust simply for being who they were. The deaths were senseless, and brutal, though, there is still hope that comes from this. It is only in understanding the past that we can build a peaceful

Introduction

future. I hope that you enjoy walking through this journey of my life.

Chapter 1:

Running for my Life

Many years ago, I never realised that my life would be a story worth telling, one that could change a life or make an impact on society. Today, I realise that my life does have a purpose borne through the challenging experience that I lived through, and survived. Here is my story, from the beginning.

My name is Regina Weinkrantz. I was born in the year 1919, in Krakow in Poland, and I lived with my 3 younger siblings – all brothers, and with my mother and father. We were a proud Jewish family, staunch in our beliefs and lifestyle. My father worked with his hands, and could repair almost anything. My mother focused on raising us children, although she did have a vegetable garden where she grew some of our food. We did not have much, but we had enough and we were never without.

I seemed to live in my own world, oblivious to what was happening beyond the borders of where I lived. My neighbourhood had people from varied cultural and ethnic backgrounds, and we all mingled with each other peacefully. It had never occurred to me that there were places where people could not live as we did, or that people could hate someone purely because of their race. I was innocent and carefree.

Chapter 1: Running for my Life

Being born after the First World War, I had grown up hearing tales from my parents of the hardship that they had experienced, but all this seemed like a fascinating past that I could not relate with. All I would think about was the shortage of food, and how awful it had been that they would eat an orange in its entirety, even including the peel. For the most part, I had grown up having everything that I needed, and almost everything that I wanted.

By the time I was entering my teenage years, my friends and I would avidly discuss our possible futures and of course, marriage. I had dreams of finding a nice well to do man, who worked hard so that I had a lovely home, and maybe two or three little children. I was still a child, with dreams of being an adult, and what it would entail. I was completing my high school education, and looking forward to finding a good job so that I could meet new people. It was difficult to find me anywhere without a big smile on my face.

That all changed one day when news came of an invasion. I had heard about the German ruler, Adolf Hitler, and his persecution of Jews in Germany, although, since it was so far away, I had never truly thought about what it meant. What I knew was that it was not possible to have a business and be successful in Germany, even if one was German. As long as they were Jewish, then they needed to look elsewhere to build up their lives. Now, I was about to face the reality. The Germans were coming into Poland, and they had one mission, to get rid of all the Jews. I was at that stage between childhood and adulthood, wanting to understand what was going on, but not fully being able to comprehend it.

Leaving Everything Behind

It was the beginning of September in 1939 when all hell seemed to break loose in our community. It seemed that something was happening in Warsaw which had everyone scurrying to find somewhere safe to go. I found this strange as I always imagined that where we lived was safe. When I looked more deeply at where the panic was coming from, I realised that it was only the Jews that were unsettled.

My parents panicked, and before I knew what had happened, they were packing up our belongings as best they could and letting us children know that we needed to flee. As the oldest, I had to help my mother put together the bare necessities, and ensure that we had enough food for a journey of several days. It seemed such an overreaction to the news of an invasion far away from us. I didn't want to leave home, or my friends. I could not quite understand why they were behaving in this way, and where were we to go anyway?

For the first time in my life that I can remember, my mother was extremely sharp with the instructions that she gave me, and refused to take the time to offer me an explanation. It was so out of character for her, especially as we had always been so close and she was patient beyond measure. Watching her behave like this sprung me to action, as it began to resonate within me that things were changing.

Having never left the place where I was born, this was a frightening thought. Although, watching the frantic way that my parents were behaving made me realise that something must really be wrong, and it would be unwise to stick around in the hope of figuring out what it could be. Despite wanting to stay, I helped pack up our things and we set off.

Chapter 1: Running for my Life

When we finally closed up the house to set off, I was alarmed to find that the entire neighbourhood had people doing the very same thing. Worried looking parents were dressed in their travelling clothes ushering their children away, and it looked as though soon the entire street would be abandoned. It was no longer just the Jews in a panic. In the few minutes that I spent packing with my family, it appeared that almost everyone had made the decision to leave. No one seemed to be talking, apart from the urgent cries to hurry up. I quickly followed my parents, not wanting to be separated from them in all the excitement.

We moved away from our home, visiting relatives many miles away. When we arrived, we found that not everyone had panicked – in fact, life was going on as usual for a vast number of people including my relatives. In their area, they were least concerned about the Germans and their invasions, as they believed that this was a political battle that would come to an end before it became a real issue. For me, this seemed like the sane way to behave, and I even questioned whether both my parents and the people in our street were fully in control of their senses. My parents decided it would be wise to temporarily settle next to our family, and for just over a year, we lived an almost carefree life. We lived as normal, although, somewhere at the back of our minds we were always alert for further news about the invasion.

Time to Move Again

Then one day, we received news that we should be prepared for an evacuation. The issues were more serious than we had anticipated, and the Germans were waging war with a whole host of other countries. They were using Poland like their backyard, as a place where they could hold their prisoners of war. There were messages that were quickly being sent all around the country.

The imminence of the arrival of the Germans was a message being spread throughout the little village that we were settled in. Though this news sounded as though it was meant to save us, something about it was amiss. From listening to years of rumours and conversations, I knew that the Germans did not have our best interests at heart, and were not to be trusted.

My family and I started to put things away and pack our belongings, wondering where we would be heading to next. Just as were becoming comfortable in a new home following new routines, we needed to get up and go somewhere else. It seemed unfair to me, and my brothers grumbled throughout the process we were packing to move. It was not an adventure anymore for them, as they knew that it might be days before we found a place to settle.

We chose to run again, and visit some of father's Polish friends who he had worked with in the past. My father's first concern was safety for all of us, and this was an attempt to ensure that we were all safe. Having established a meaningful friendship, he was sure that we would be welcomed into their home.

Arriving at their home, we were welcomed, although just for the night. There was a considerable amount of anti-Semitic propaganda going around and the people we were to stay with were not Jewish. They were afraid of what would happen to them if it was discovered that they were keeping six Jews in their home. My father understood, although I could tell that he was also at a loss as to what he should do, or where to go to next. As a family, we decided to face the next day together, and figure out a solution.

Chapter 1: Running for my Life

That night, we ate a silent meal, every one of us contemplating the future and trying to understand what it would mean. My father and his friend started a discussion, wondering if perhaps the best thing that we could do was leave the country. We were warned against trying to do so, as it seemed the Germans had truly spread themselves out, and one of the more dangerous places we could be would be near the borders.

They discussed the resettlement, where Jews were being sent to live in new places, as the Germans took over their old properties. It was the first time that I heard the phrase concentration camp. It sounded like a place where Jews were sent to work for the Germans for little pay to help with the war efforts. It seemed that more than anything, my father wanted to war to be over so that we could safely return home.

As we went to sleep that night, we could hear the screams, gunshots and loud voices of the German soldiers looking for the Jews. I was confused, as I expected them to simply come and move us from where we were to the settlement areas. The voices seemed to be coming closer and closer, and I could feel my body completely tense up and perspiration run down my forehead. For the first time, the invasion seemed real to me. I began to understand why there was so much fear. Try as I did, my heart would not stop racing. We huddled together as a family, leaning on each other for love, support and the reassurance that everything was going to be alright. It was in this huddle that we spent the night, all of us sleeping for short periods and fitfully, all waiting to hear that the soldiers had gone past out door.

Our hosts did not get much sleep either, as they were keeping watch next to the windows, to warn us if they saw any of the soldiers coming to the door. We were scared, and so were they.

It was one of the longest nights that I have ever experienced in my life.

Chapter 2:

Living in Hiding

That night, we managed to escape the radar of the blood thirsty Germans. As each moment passed, I would hear my mother mumbling, silently praying to Yahweh to keep us safe, and thanking him for his protection in each moment. When morning came, my father thanked our hosts profusely, and they sent us on our way to the next destination, with food to last all six of us a few days. I could almost see the relief in their eyes when they were letting us go, and I could not blame them. The terrifying sounds of the soldiers were still ringing in my ears. My mother had tears in her eyes as we left, not because she was miserable, but because she was amazed that there were still people who could be so kind in times that were so challenging.

My father had another friend whom we were to try and stay with, although this friend was also a Jew. As we made our way to our new residing place, we hoped and prayed that we would still find it standing. Luckily, we arrived safely and found that it was still amongst the few places that had a sizeable Jewish population. It was clear that there were some people who were determined to go on living as normal, no matter what the threats to their existence may be.

Chapter 2: Living in Hiding

My parents wanted us to get back to living as normal too, so that the war and the persecution of Jews would not affect us in any way. It was not that they were denying what was happening all around us, I think it was also to protect their own sanity, and help mask the fear that they were experiencing. Luckily, the new place we went to had a small home that was available, so we were close to my father's Jewish friends, and we were also able to enjoy the privacy of our own home again. All of us children shared a bedroom, but that did not affect us at all. We were just relieved to be safe.

Thus my younger brothers were registered to attend the local school, while I was to find an odd job to help with the household. It quickly became apparent that their plans were not going to be in any successful. To begin with, my brothers were immediately thrown out of school the moment it was realised that they were Jews.

This was saddening for my brothers, but I believe, it was also a blessing in disguise. The education system at the time was fully in control of the Nazis, and it was heavy with propaganda. Before long, the teachers started wearing the Nazi uniforms and became members of the Nazi party, which made it unsafe to be Jewish and want to learn at this time.

My father took note of the problem and registered my brothers in an all Jewish school that had just come up within our community. Finally, they were able to get an education, as all the teachers and students were Jewish within the school. However, they were not saved from bullying from German children while at school. In the evenings, members of a group of children who proudly called themselves Hitler's youth would spend their time outside the school, waiting for the students to come out. Most of the time they would simply jeer at them, and hurl insults. As time went on they begun to spit at the student, and then it escalated into full violence.

There was nothing that the authorities could do, as they had no interest in Jewish children. The Jewish authorities did not want to stir up any more trouble, especially as the war was going on and we knew that all Jews were subject to being persecuted. In fact, for them it may have caused an international incident of sorts, including continuous physical fights amongst the children. My brothers were told that they would have to bear it for a while, and that they should never raise a fist or speak a violent word against the German children. It seemed so unfair at the time, but there was nothing that could be done about it.

Anywhere I went to look for a job I ended up with either a door slammed in my face, or a face full of spit. My father was facing the same issue, as no one wanted to hire him at all. In a way, it was an even worse experience for him. As the person who provided for our family, resorting to asking the neighbours for assistance, even for the most simple of meals, would wear away at his soul.

One day when he was on the train, he was viciously attacked and beaten, not because he had done anything, simply because he was Jewish. At the time, he had been travelling to look for some work which he heard was available several miles away. When they were done beating him, they threw him out of the train, and he broke his arm. By the time he made it home, we did not know what to do next. I was angry inside, and I wanted to go out and get revenge on the evil people who had done this to him. I will never forget my father's reaction to my anger. He told me that it was not my place to fight for him, that we should leave it to God. No matter what would happen to us, all would be in God's hands. That evening, I had to change my attitude. Instead of being continuously upset, I decided to thank God for his mercies, and for bringing back my father alive.

Things Get Worse

By this time, I firmly believed that things could not get any worse than they were at the moment. We had next to nothing as a family, everyone was tense and miserable, and between us, we experienced fits of temper. The loving joyous childhood that I had so casually taken for granted was coming to an end. I was extremely wrong. The changes that had once been subtle, were no longer subtle in the community where we lived. As Jews, we were outsiders of the worst kind, and were really being looked down upon.

All the business that were owned by Jews had been closed down, so many of our neighbours did not have any income coming in. It was too dangerous to travel far away, as there were still tales of Jews disappearing and never being found again. We knew what was going on, but there was still so much that was unknown. It was the unknown that terrified us the most.

A few weeks after my father's incident on the train, I spotted some posters that had been plastered all over town. These posters said that Jews were no longer allowed to travel in vehicles any longer, whether these were public or private. This meant that we could no longer use the train, or even a carriage if we wanted to move from one point to another. The only option that we had was to walk everywhere.

All around me were people from different nationalities, and religions. It seemed surreal that only the Jews were being targeted. As I read this notice, I could almost feel the eyes of curious onlookers observing me. I figured they wanted to see some reaction from me.

I felt as though I had been deflated, like someone had truly knocked the wind out of me. This community was supposed to save us, and help us to live. Now more and more people were starting to move away, just as we had when we left our home and finally ended up here. The problem that we had is that there was nowhere else for us to go. This was our final destination.

I ran home and could not control the tears that were running down my face. I did not care who saw me in this state of distress, or what their opinion of my state was. I needed to speak to my parents, I needed answers from them. When I made it home, I asked my father and my mother why this was happening to us. What was so terrible about being a Jew that people treated us like we had a nasty disease? I wanted to know why they did not want us around anymore.

My father reacted in anger, and scolded me for looking down upon myself. He told me that there was nothing wrong with who we were and what we believed in. That we were God's people, and he cared for us. We were never to be ashamed, and we should always hold our heads up high no matter what was to happen.

My mother was holding on to me as he said these things, with his eyes flashing and his entire face a bright beet red. I had never seen him this angry before, and I found myself wiping my tears and resolving within me that I need to take pride in being Jewish. I needed to, so that I would survive and not allow my soul to give in to the grim circumstances that were surrounding us each day.

Chapter 2: Living in Hiding

The Jewish family who had taken us in were beginning to feel the weight of war on their shoulders. Even though they were Jewish, a quick look at them facially revealed their 'Aryan' like features. When the Germans come, if they had the courage to, they could claim not to be Jewish and there was a chance that they would be spared from what was awaiting us all. Everyone in our family however, had curly hair and dark eyes. We stood out and could not deny our heritage.

The Germans were getting closer and closer, and we could tell that our hosts were becoming more nervous about having us in their village, especially because we were living there on their recommendation. This meant that when the Nazis started asking questions, we could be traced back to them putting us all in jeopardy. My father needed to make a rapid alternative decision, and he did. It was for us to pack up our things and run away again. Even though we did not know where we were to be going, we packed up our things, profusely thanked our hosts for giving us a chance at life again and set out.

We wandered around the outskirts of the village, but within a short time we could clearly hear the wail of a siren. There was no turning back now. The Nazis were upon us.

Chapter 3:

Caught, and trapped

One thing that brought total terror to our thoughts was the possibility of being caught by the Einsatzgruppen. There had been rumours flying all over the village we were staying, about these task forces and the danger of travelling with them. The rumour was that people who got trapped within them, never made it to their destination. I was terrified of that I would fall to the same fate, so the closer the sounds of the Nazi soldiers, the more that fear seemed to grip me entire being.

By now, we could see the dust storms from their vehicles travelling around the village, and hear the stamping of their feet as they marched from door to door. We were yet to see them face to face but they were so close in sound, that we knew it would only be moments before we finally saw our captors first hand.

My parents realised that there was no point in trying to run away any more. In doing so, we were bringing more harm than good to the people who made the decision to help us. We took our belongings some way away from the home of his friend and continued with our trek although it was futile and before long, we were spotted by the German police. Therefore, we were caught.

Chapter 3: Caught, and trapped

The day we were caught is imprinted in my memory. It was a Tuesday afternoon, and we could hear the soldiers coming. With nowhere to run, we sat together, holding hands and praying while we waited for the inevitable. They had already signalled to us and told us we should not run. When they came to get us, they separated us, leaving me with my mother and my father with my brothers. We were all given these yellow stars to wear, which would let everyone who saw them immediately know that we were Jewish.

At the time, I thought that the separation was for the purpose of transporting us to our next destination. For a while, I had my father and brothers within view but then they were led away and I could not see them anymore. I clung to my mother, more from wondering what was going to happen next, than from any real and palpable fear.

Looking around, I realised that it was not only the Jews that were being arrested. I saw people from many nationalities, and even some Germans as well. Apparently, they were part of the undesirable in society, and thus, they were to be captured like the rest of us. They were being carried out of bushes and places where they had hidden along the road, and I even spotted a few people who had been living with us in our little village.

Transported to the Ghetto

While we were being put together with all the other people, and the Nazis were collecting other Jews, I asked my mother what would happen if we said that we were Christians. I thought that by doing so we would be saved. I knew that my father had told us to be proud of who we were but I could not shake the fear that was threatening to completely come over me. At the time, this seemed like an excellent idea. However, my mother said that it would be impossible for such a plan to work. Only those whose grandparents had become Christians prior to the founding of the German Empire in 1871 would be considered Christian instead of Jewish. Added to that, our distinct Jewish features would give us away, and we would be seen as liars before God.

At that time, the Germans needed us to cooperate more than they wanted us to kick up a fight. Therefore, we were being spoken to respectfully and in low tones. This was surprising as I had expected to hear the screams and shouts that I associated with the Germans, but in this instance, that was not to be the case.

We were told by a German official that we should not worry, we were being resettled to an area where there were many Jews, and we would be safe. My mother thought it wise to cooperate so we would not come to any harm, she whispered to me that soon, we will re-join my father and brothers. This helped build up some of my confidence, and I even had a little spring in my step. Now we were going to be able to live in peace because wherever the Germans were taking us would be somewhere that they controlled.

The official asked us to note which, from the pile of property were our possessions, as these would be returned to us once we arrived at our new dwelling. I quickly did a visual check and was able to identify our cases which contained our clothes and food. I hoped that the food would withstand the journey we were about to take because I was beginning to feel some hunger pangs. It almost seemed as though we were preparing to go on a holiday somewhere, but the sinister expressions of the officers, and the terrified glances from the people told a different story. I suddenly realised that I was weary of their intentions.

Chapter 3: Caught, and trapped

There was a large lorry that was driving around, picking up anyone who they came across that were Jewish or undesirable. For a second I wondered whether this would be the task force that everyone dreaded so much, but I did not have a chance to decide what I would do if it was. Once the truck reached the place where my mother and I were, we had no choice but to get into the truck and be taken to some destination.

My mother and I were bundled into this lorry with a whole host of other people. We were too close together, it was hot, and for some time, I found it difficult to catch my breath. As the lorry proceeded on its journey, all I could hope was that we arrived at whatever our destination was meant to be soon. We travelled in this truck for an entire day and an entire night. It was uncomfortable and at some point, I wondered about whether we would actually get to any destination. Before I knew it, we had halted, and in front of us was the train station.

What made this situation even more trying and challenging to understand was the way all the different events played out. For so long, I had heard about how terrible the Germans were, and how they were busy killing all the people. The way they were speaking to us as they rounded us up seemed normal, as though we were all of the same understanding and were moving towards a familiar goal. Yes, we had experienced some discomfort travelling in the truck, but it had not been enough to fully traumatise me. This was the deception that they used to capture such a large number of us Jews.

Arriving at the Ghetto

The next thing was being shipped off to one of the ghettos. It was true we were to be resettled, and I had been ignorant about what the ghetto represented or what the conditions could be like. This is because they had sprung up as a result of the war, and I had never experienced anything like a ghetto as I was growing up. I therefore did not experience fear, just curiosity as to what my new home would look like. This far, we had not been harmed so I was not afraid. We were all placed onto a train, and found a place to sit in one of the freight cars. There was no stopping, and no place to relieve oneself. It took several hours before we reached our destination, the ghetto, our new home.

I had never seen anything like this place before. It was full of people, all desperate and miserable, trying to make sense out of their situation. There were sick people who had open sores, thin people who looked like they had not eaten in weeks and people who seemed to have no spirit left within them. Almost everyone looked as though they had been severely starved, and for a while I wondered whether it had reached a point where someone would want to eat me. I clung to my mother, seeking her love and support but from her facial expression I could tell that she too was trying to figure out how she would adjust.

In our first night at the ghetto, we were taken together with the party that we had travelled with to a single room to get some sleep. This was because we had arrived late in the day, and would be processed the following day. There were not beds or tables, or any proper surfaces where we could lay our heads. That night, I slept in my mother's arms in a tiny space, terrified, but glad that she was by my side.

When we woke up the next day, the hell I thought I was in turned out to be an illusion because things were about to become much worse, very quickly. We were allocated a small apartment, which barely had any amenities or space for that matter. When we arrived at the apartment, we found that we needed to share the space with four other families. To protect our belongings, a meagre cup, plate and spoon, we decided to sleep on them or to hide them strategically under the bed. We were cold at night, but had no heating, and nothing to cover our bodies with. Food was scarce, as we were given enough just to stay alive, but not to build our strength. All around us were police, Jewish police, forced to keep us under control. They were known as the Judenrat, and they followed all the demands of the Nazis. I found it cowardly that the Nazis did not have someone to take care of their dirty work.

I was surprised to find that within the ghetto, there were groups of us, groups of Jews who had formed secret organisations that were meant to defend us. These groups spoke of freedom, overcoming the enemy and of final freedom and liberation. I wanted to join one of them so much, but I did not have the heart to. I was afraid that if something were to happen to me, I would leave my mother on her own, which would surely bring her own life to an end. My focus turned to surviving each day, finding the means to feed myself and my mother, and staying alive. Over time, I had become an expert at ensuring that everything we needed was available.

Having not realised that there were people being killed as a part of the invasion, I held on to the hope of finding the other members of my family. I spent time searching for my father and my brothers, although this was in vain. No matter where I looked, or whom I dared to ask, no-one had seen them, and in most cases, they were not even willing to answer me.

This did not mean that I gave up hope. The ghetto that we were in was large, and I came up with a plan of how I could canvas the entire area within a certain period, so that I could discover if my family were there. It was when my plan came underway that yet again, my course of my life took another turn and everything changed.

Leaving the Ghetto

For some reason, a large group of us were told that it was time for us to leave the ghetto. We were needed elsewhere, where we were to be given new life.

My mother and I were put together with a large group of other Jews and told that we needed to get ready for a journey. We were to leave Poland and make our way into Germany. As much as I wanted to leave the ghetto, I was not ready to go to Germany, as I believed it to be the land of our enemy.

To get ready for the trip, my mother wanted to make sure that we had some sustenance to eat, especially as we did not know how long the journey would be. She also wanted us to have something warm for us to wear, so that we would not be overcome with the elements.

As we were getting ready to leave, the Germans started to count us. In total, they reached around 950 people who were to travel that day. We seemed like a large number, and one would think that we would be difficult to control. But by this time, we were so weak, tired and exhausted from the mistreatment, that we would willingly do anything that was asked of us, if only so that we could stay alive for a day longer.

By this time, I was sure that I would not see my brothers or father again, but I did not have time to mourn. Although I had tried to go through a large amount of the apartments in the ghetto, none of them revealed that there was any knowledge of my fathers and brothers existence in the place. There were still a few more placed to check, though almost all my efforts seemed fruitless.

Chapter 3: Caught, and trapped

I began begging with my mother, going from door to door asking for whatever little food or water that others could spare. We managed to get just enough for a day. By collecting two threadbare and worn sheets, we even managed to find something that we could use to cover ourselves when we were cold. We set out with the rest of the group.

We believed that we were being led somewhere so that we could work as labourers. We had heard of Jewish tailors who were now making uniforms for the Nazi soldiers, while other men were sent off to work in mines or factories. My mother and I had resigned ourselves to this fate, believing that our portion was to be slave labour for the war efforts.

When we were coming to the ghetto, we were transported on a train. Now, there was no train, wagon or other transportation in sight. My mother and I walked for three days, and then we arrived at our destination. We had not been taken to Germany as we were told. In my mind at the time, this was a relief. We were still in our native land, in surroundings that could be deemed familiar. Instead of being in Germany, we were at a concentration camp. Auschwitz.

Chapter 4:

Survival of the Fittest

I had heard about the concentration camps, though I had not imagined that I would ever be in one. There were so many different types, including labour camps, extermination camps, prisoner of war camps and even camps for police detention. I recalled the conversation that I heard about the concentration camps and thought to myself that I have finally been able to see a resettlement area. This was a new one, so close to the town of my birth. Auschwitz was to be my new home. From the outside, it looked like a typical settlement, there were barbed wire fences and a new building that we were walking towards. From this point of view, the place resembled a labour camp above all else. The camp had only been in existence for a few months, so the surroundings were relatively good.

The camp itself was quite huge, covering a total area of 40 square kilometres. There were three sections of the camp. There was the place that was the base camp and it also had the central office, and this part was called Auschwitz 1. Then there was the part that I was sent to, the second part of the camp. It was called Auschwitz 2, or Auschwitz Birkenau. Then there was the Auschwitz 3 which was the third part of the camp. It actually resembled a sub-camp and it was also referred to as

Chapter 4: Survival of the Fittest

Monoscwitz. The camp had 28 buildings in all the three sections.

The reason that I believed that Auschwitz was a labour camp was because of the words that were painted boldly over the main entrance. They read "Arbeit Macht Frei", which translates to work will give you freedom. This gave me some hope of what I was going to experience. In my mind, this place would give my mother and I a chance to work hard so that we could find our way back home to my father and my brothers. We would no longer be prisoners of the Germans, and would be free, just as we had always been. Even after all that I had experienced to date, my mind still had the naïveté and innocence that you would find in a young child.

I still had the fear of the unknown coursing through my veins, and wondered whether life would be anything like the ghetto we just left. As my mother and I walked in, hands clasped tightly together as if we were a life line for each other, there were men dressed in stripes everywhere. Together with those who had travelled with us, we stood in a line, confused, hungry and exhausted. One of the Germans who was dressed in uniform was putting us into groups. He took one look at me, and then at my mother, and immediately separated us. I screamed, I shouted, I begged but it was no use. The last member of my family was taken away from me, and I was powerless to stop it. I never saw my mother again. It was years later that I learnt she did not survive to the end of that day.

I never had to time to carry on with my tirade following the separation as I was quickly threatened with the butt of a gun. If I continued making any more noise or causing a commotion, I would be killed. I pulled myself together, trying to find within me a strength that I was sure did not exist. It was initially strange for me to be separated from my mother as I had always considered myself to be her little girl. I watched as other children were left with their mothers, and I envied them and wished that I was them.

The group that I was in had people who were young, like me. For the Germans, this meant that we were more likely to live, and would be useful if we were to be put to work. I was only 22 years old at the time, a young adult learning to leave the mind-set of a little girl behind. I had grown up innocent and safe, and did not have the tools to survive in such a situation. I found myself in another line, where I was given my own striped clothes. Now I matched all those who had found they were to live in this place.

Then someone came up to me with a razor and sheared off all my hair. My dark blond curls that were once my pride and joy now lay at my feet, taken away from me without my consent. I felt stripped and helpless. Then, a number was crudely tattooed onto my left arm. I stood there, bald with sharp cuts in my head, pain in my arm, no possessions except the uniform in a small, crowded room with a cold floor. I had ceased to be a real person in the eyes of the Germans. I was one of a multitude – a number.

My First Day in the Concentration Camp

I looked around and saw another girl, and it was like looking in the mirror. She also appeared to be in shock, and dejected from what was happening to us. I spoke to her, and found out her name was Elka. That day we formed a union, I cannot call it friendship for the circumstances were too bleak for that, it was more like an alliance, a way to help each other survive.

Chapter 4: Survival of the Fittest

Most of those who had been left to survive, the people who were in our group, were to offer forced labour to the Germans. The men were given physically demanding tasks, which required them to be active outdoors in all types of weather, and to carry out tasks that could physically impair one who was not strong and fit.

For us women, our fate was much worse than one could imagine. There was a rule that had been laid out by the Nazis, especially when it came to Jewish women. No one was supposed to marry us or have any children with us. There was no room for any babies that carried mixed blood in what was to become the new Germany.

This however, did not stop us from being 'broken in' by the soldiers that were in the camp. The very first day, even before we were taken to the quarters that we were to stay in, Elka and I and most of the other young girls in my group were separated from the rest of the women. We were led into a room, and suddenly, the room filled with soldiers. We were terrified and tried to huddle together, knowing that letting out a scream would result in our death.

The men grabbed one of the girls that was next to us. She struggled which we found out to be her biggest mistake. They took of her striped clothes so that she was in front of us all, completely naked. Then I watched slowly as they took off their own trousers, four of the in total, and proceeded to rape her. Her screams rang out and then the next four soldiers came when the others were spent. They did the same thing, took off their trousers but this time, the sodomised her. She screamed until all that was coming out of her mouth was a rasping and gasping sound. When they were done, they let in what appeared to be a mad dog which mauled her until there was no sound coming from her. After this, they urinated on her and kicked her to the side. We were all completely dumbfounded, and stood and watched.

The soldiers said that if we looked away, we would be punished. When they were done with her, they told us that this was a warning. Unless we agreed to intercourse, we would suffer the same fate. Resistance was not permitted, and screaming meant death.

We all had to take off our clothes and lie down, as the soldiers used our bodies as objects for their own satisfaction. By the time I had left the room, I had been used by three soldiers, all with different levels of brutality. As a virgin, I had never experienced anything like this before and words could not describe the pain that I was in.

Slowly, we limped into our quarters where we were to spend the night. I longed for the arms of my mother to hold me, and most of the other girls were whimpering softly. I felt helpless and completely powerless. If the Nazis were looking for a way to break my will, then they had managed.

I began to take notice of the other women who were around me, and realised that they all had a knowing look. Some of them had bandages around their breasts, which had been cut off for their resistance. It was too much for me to take in that one evening, my first day at this awful place. I fell into a fitful sleep that night.

Moving Forward at the Concentration Camp

The next day I was awoken, and I felt extremely battered and bruised. There was some blood coming out of my private parts, but I had no way of checking to see the damage. It was different from my menses, and I figured out how to fold a small cloth to keep the bleeding concealed.

First thing in the morning, we were all taken outside. I was wary of where we were going, and wondered if I was to experience more of what had happened the first day. All around me were men and women of different ages, getting into orderly lines so that they could start the day. I watched what everyone was doing and imitated them so that I would not stand out as odd.

It was then that I noticed there were no children anywhere. All the children that we had come with had disappeared with their mothers, never to be seen again. I later found out that all the children had been ordered dead, so that they would not have the chance to grow up and create an entirely new generation of Jews.

The living conditions in the camp were possibly worse than what I had experienced in the ghetto. Whereas I had complained about there being minimal space in the ghetto, the camp offered less than half of what we had there. Sometimes, we would be so crowded when we were to sleep in the wooden bunks that we would have to figure out how three of us could fit on a space that was meant for one person.

The reason that the bunks were so small was because they had been modelled to resemble horse stables. There were 250 barracks in total in the Birkenau part of Auschwitz. When counting the spaces in each barrack, they came up to a total of 52. Had we been horses, they would have taken only 52 of us in each. Unfortunately, we were Jews, and not subject to the same luxury treatment of the horses. On any given day, we would be between 800 and 1000 people in each of the barracks. To say that we were overcrowded would be making an understatement. I had long lost any hope of experiencing privacy and comfort in my life again.

Before each work day, the soldiers who were stationed at our camp were meant to carry out a headcount. This was to be done every day, no matter what the weather could be. Almost every morning as this headcount took place, I would carry out another headcount in my own head. I would count the number of dead bodies that were on the fence for the day. In the middle of the night, many people plotted and planned their escapes, and would try to jump over the fences. The fences were double barbed wire, and they were electrical. A single touch and the jumper would be completed electrocuted until they died. Escape was futile.

Elka and I were given work to do, everyday sorting through piles of clothes, arranging and packing them. Sometimes, we would go through personal items, things that looked as though they were once precious to someone, and had now been relegated to a heap. I remembered my own possessions and those of our family that we were to receive in the ghetto. They never came back to us, and were possibly being sorted out the same way.

Our typical work day took 12 hours, and we were given a short break at noon, where we were given a watery soup, sometimes with a floating piece of carrot, to keep us going for the rest of the work. We were to work from dawn to dusk, and when we were not working, we were subjected to hours standing upright during the daily head counts.

When we were sorting out, we were to follow some strict instructions. We had to go through the pockets of all the items, checking to see if there were any valuables to be found there. Valuables, especially gold, jewellery and money were to be put aside for the Nazis. We were also to cut out any fur that was lining coats and put these aside as well. Where there were clothes that had layers, we were given scissors so that we could cut through the layers to check whether there were any valuable items hidden inside.

Every item seemed to tell a story, even though we had no idea who they belonged to. There were more and more items to go through each day. The work was endless. We found out that these were the possessions of victims who had been exterminated, fellow Jews and other prisoners like us who had lost our lives. Going through their things affected us psychologically, especially as it brought to reality that so many of them were likely dead and would never see their families again. This filled me with deep sadness, but also gave me hope for the future, as I was still alive.

The Germans had many ways of fighting against the Jews. They took away our possessions, took away our homes, mistreated our physical bodies, and tried to rip our hearts and souls away from us. This was the one part of me I was determined not to let them have. Despite all the awful things that I had been subjected to, the things that I had seen and experienced, I told myself that I would not allow a German to have my heart or my soul. I remembered the words of my father, that this was not my fight. I was to leave it all up to God and have faith that eventually justice would be done.

My Revelation of Impending Death

Gladly, Elka and I were never again taken to the room where the soldiers raped us on that first day. It seemed that there were so many new people coming in each day, they had fresh pickings and did not need to use our bodies any more. This did not take away the pain of what had happened, but it was a welcome relief.

Now, we were stationed to continue working all day, and we were moved in different areas within the camp to carry out our work.

Almost every day, when we looked out into the sky, we would see huge plumes of smoke. For a time, I wondered what was being disposed of each day, such that there would be so much smoke and ash. I slowly realised what is was when the air was full of the smell from burning flesh. As there were no animals around, I knew that thousands of people were cremated each day. I did not want to think of those who ended up in these massive fires. I convinced myself that they must have been those who were weak and did not make it, dying of natural (if you can call what we were going through natural) causes. I refused to permit my mind to consider that there were people who were deliberately murdered and killed in this way.

Sometimes, the plumes of smoke would disappear, and it also seemed that many people would also disappear within a day of arriving at the camp. These disappearances had no explanation, it was almost magical to me the way the people would suddenly vanish. I would see them being walked through the camp, although most of the time they had not yet been given their striped uniforms. Within the camp, there were large rooms that were separated by gates. During the day, new arrivals were often led through the gate that was close to where our sleeping chamber was. I would watch them walk through the gates, and they would never walk out. A new group of people would walk into the rooms ever twenty or so minutes. Now I understand that they were being led to their death in a gas chamber.

Chapter 4: Survival of the Fittest

These gated rooms were four in total. Above each day were signs. Some of them said 'Bath and Disinfecting Rooms', whereas the other signs said 'Cleanliness beings freedom.' I suppose they were meant to give the people who were being marched into them a false sense of security as to what they would find once they entered the rooms. On a busy day, there would be plumes of smoke coming out of all four of them. When the wind would blow the smoke in my direction, I would occasionally catch the whiff of burnt hair. I could not allow myself to think about what this meant.

Time seemed to move and stand still all at once. The days went by and Elka and I carried out the same routine, always in silence. I was actually thankful for the work that I was given to do. Compared to what I had seen of the camp, my work was generally easy, more physically than emotionally. It allowed me to build up my strength, and slowly, I began to feel the tingle of hope rising within me.

Chapter 5:

The Horror that was my Reality

Elka and I had managed to get ourselves into a routine, where the days seemed to blend into each other, such that we had an expectation of what we were likely to face from one moment to the next. Having this helped to keep us sane, especially considering all the insane things that were happening around us. We soon learnt that there was nothing that could hide us from the torture, the pain and the horror. This realisation came to us suddenly, and we were forced to face a new reality.

Experiments, and Pain

One day, our routine changed. Men in white coats who we recognised as physicians from Germany, came and picked a group of young girls from the crowd. Elka and I were amongst those that were chosen. With no choice, we followed our captors, and wondered what our fate would be. In this place, death did not require you to do something wrong, or provoke anyone. It appeared to us that the Germans killed for sport, or to instil fear in others. We were taken away from everyone else, into separate rooms. No one spoke to us, or let us know what was happening, though they did speak extensively amongst themselves.

Chapter 5: The Horror that was my Reality

A number of men in white coats came into the room. A physician named Schumann (I overheard him being called by one of his colleagues) looked us over, ensuring that we were healthy. He asked us only one question, 'Are you Jewish?' to which we both nodded yes. Despite everything that had happened to the Jewish people, I remained proud of my heritage and had promised myself that I would never denounce it. Elka and I were taken into a large room, together with some of the other women. We were to become the subjects of medical experimentation.

It was at this point that fear kicked into me, and before I could stop myself I was screaming and trying to get out of the place we were being held as quickly as possible. I was later restrained for my efforts, and the procedure that I was to go through was scheduled. I was truly afraid of what would become of me.

That very day, the experiments started. Every few moments, one of the women was taken from the room. It seemed that every person would have a turn to find out what was happening. Then suddenly my turn came. I glanced at Elka who was still waiting, and wondered if I would ever see her again. I was led into a room and asked to lie down on a bench. There was strange equipment all around me, and I realised that it was an X-ray machine.

I had heard of them, and thought them to be harmless. I knew that they took pictures of bones, and helped doctors see inside the human body. I should have known that my captors would not have my best interests at heart. The X-Ray machine began to scan my body, focusing on what seemed to be my lower belly. At first, I felt nothing, just a slight warmth, but within a few minutes, this had turned into searing pain. It was as though something was being ripped out of me, something within me was dying. I was being dangerously affected by the radiation that comes from the X-ray machine.

I knew I could not risk jumping off the bench in protest, as such behaviour was enough to get someone shot. Neither could I cry out in pain as the result would also be disastrous. I had to bear the pain, hoping and praying that it would be over soon. When the machine was done with the scanning, I looked down and saw that my entire belly was bright red, and burned. It was so painful, I could not even bring myself to touch it. I was told I could leave the room, and holding the wall for support, I made my way out of there. I found out years later that this incident ruined my ovaries. I was one of the statistics, one who was a victim of the mass sterilisation of the Jews.

I ended up being led to another room, one where there were other women, and even some men, in a condition similar to my own. All I could do was sit down in a corner and wait for the pain to go away. After what seemed like hours, Elka joined me in the room. We were united again, this time, sharing our physical pain. We were taken to a place for healing, where every day, the physician would come and take a look at us. We were not given any medicine at all. Some people got infections and died, while others like me, got better slowly, our skin healing, with painful scars left behind. When it seemed I was adequately healed, it was time to return to my daily duties in the camp.

Elka had been sent back a few days before me. When the officer in charge told me it was time to leave, I started to walk towards the door. I was told I needed to be searched before I could leave. I wondered what I could possibly have that they would need to search me for. I had no choice but to comply.

Chapter 5: The Horror that was my Reality

A male officer asked me to take off all my clothing. I did, and he looked at the scars on my belly that went all the way around. Flashbacks of my first day in the camp came to mind, and I waited for the room to fill up with soldiers. I knew that I would be too weak to fight them off on account of my wounds and my scars, and now, my hope was that they would tire quickly and finish up with me.

I waited to hear the patter of other feet, and I waited to be told to lie down. Neither of these things happened. Instead, the one soldier then asked me to bend over forwards, so that my arms dangled above my feet. He conducted an invasive search on me, checking to see if there was anything that I had hidden in my private parts. Although it was uncomfortable, it was not as bad as having man after man on top of you, using your body for their own pleasure. I dared not shed a tear, cry or show my fear or revulsion. I knew he wanted to degrade me and humiliate me. I refused to give him the satisfaction. When he was done, I was ordered to dress and leave. At that point, I would have wholeheartedly welcomed death.

A New Job

After being released from the place where I was being held for these experiments, I was given a new job. Due to my weakened state, I was deemed as not strong enough to continue with the work that I had been given in the past, even though that work had proven to not be particularly challenging.

I found myself taken to a large room within the camp, I room I had always seen people going into, but never coming out of. When I stepped inside the room, I understood why. All around me were corpses, of people who had died just that day. I felt my stomach retching, but nothing came out, as there was nothing there. All I did was cough out air, though it was painful and I had to get it under control quickly before I found myself looking down the barrel of a gun.

Almost all the corpses were completely naked, with just a few still wearing their normal clothing. Some of the bodies were still warm, indicating that they had only been there for a short while. The moment I had finished my job, they would all be carried into a large furnace room where they would be collectively cremated and their ashes scattered on the ground. So much ash had been scattered and mixed into the ground that it was not grey instead of red, as most of the soil was made up of fragments of bone.

My job was to go through as many dead bodies as possible, to check their mouth for gold teeth. Some of them had been already marked by the Nazis before they were placed in the gas chambers. It appeared that when they were lining up to be sent into the chambers, the soldiers would check their mouths to determine whether they had gold teeth or not. To be sure that I did not miss out on any of the teeth, I was told to check all of the bodies. If I was to find gold teeth in any of them, I was given a set of pliers and a small bag. I was to pull them out and collect them in the bag. I was revolted and wanted so badly to be amongst the dead. I had no choice. I had to carry out the task.

I remained in the room for six hours, going from body to body, checking and collecting teeth. In the beginning, I tried to offer up a prayer for each person that I would check, but in the end, it had proven too challenging as there were so many people. I told myself that I would pray for everyone once it was over. As the bodies were lying on top of each other, they soon started to smell and by the time I was to leave the room, the smell had become overwhelming.

Chapter 5: The Horror that was my Reality

Around three hours into the pulling out of these teeth, Elka was brought in to the room to join me. By this time, I had established a system to help me get through the work faster. As we always did, our eyes spoke for us. I saw in hers complete fear and revulsion, I hoped that she would see courage when she looked at mine. I don't think she even noticed when a tear escaped from her eye.

Like in other places in the camp, there was no possibility of escaping from the horror that was within this chamber. To keep us in line as we did our work, there were guards patrolling who carried automatic weapons and were accompanied by attach dogs. I believe that they were also meant to deter us from trying to steal anything as it was obvious that doing so would result in our death.

Eating To Survive

All around me there were people dying of starvation as our captors did not make food easily or readily available. People in this camp were from all walks of life, including those who had been rich at some points and were used to the finer things in life, and people from villages that were very small and self-sufficient.

So when it came to the food that was available, even though it was minimal, some people could not take to it at all. In preparing bread, most of the time the primary ingredient was sawdust rather than flour. Old dying horses were killed, and their meat was used to make sausages, and tea was brewed using whatever weeds were readily available. Having a meal with all these three elements was almost like having a feast.

I watched as desperate people around me had started going through the Nazi's garbage in the hope of finding some food to eat, even if the food they wanted was rotten. I simple used to hold my breath and quickly eat the bread and tea that was available. I only ate this food as I was determined to stay alive.

Eaten Alive

Apart from enduring what seemed to be unending torture at the hands of the guards and the conditions, we also had other enemies amongst us that made life a living hell. Our sleeping areas were infested with bed bugs and lice, so that even when I tried to get some sleep at night, it would be a challenge to do so.

In the beginning, I would try and scratch them off as they sucked away at my blood but as time went on, and my skin became harder, I became used to the pain that they caused me. On more than one occasion, I was woken up in the middle of the night after being bitten by a rat. There was not much room to move, and it somehow gave me solace that everyone around me was experiencing the same pain and discomfort. Not that it was something we talked about, but it did give me a feeling of solidarity in suffering with my fellow prisoners.

When I returned to what had become my normalcy in the camp (after all the experiments I had undergone), I noticed that things had changed. Most of the faces were new, and there were certainly more people than when I was sent to the experimentation room. There was serious overcrowding, and although hundreds were disappearing each day, and the plumes of smoke never abated, there were still so many people.

Chapter 5: The Horror that was my Reality

It was a few days before I was informed that I would be leaving with the next group of people. Elka and I were being transported to another camp. We noticed that the group of us who were leaving were injured, spent, and older. We no longer made up the strong youthful group that was not taking over. I knew then that wherever we were being sent, it would not be a good place to be in.

Chapter 6:

Life in the Death Camp

uschwitz was terrible, so much so that Elka and I were relieved the day we were herded out and ordered to start marching to a new camp. There was trepidation as we knew our physical condition did not make us the most appealing of Jewish prisoners, though we hoped that things would be a little better than they were at the camp. We needed to hang onto some hope, even though the reality was bleak.

We were moving to Majdanek, what we thought at the time was another concentration camp. I experienced relief when we began our long march, not because I knew anything of the destination, but because of the chance to breathe in fresh air. In the concentration camp, the air was rank with disease and human waste, making it difficult to breathe most of the time. If this smell abated, there was still the smell of constantly burning flesh as people were being cremated. Many people claimed to have gotten used to the stench, I never did. It hang over me like a suffocating blanket, and I could never get the stench off my skin.

During the march, the weather was not good, and the cold slowed many people down. I kept moving forward as the moment a person fell out of line or collapsed from exhaustion, there was always a Nazi at the ready with a loaded gun to shoot them down. Once they were shot, they would simply be kicked out of the way to make room for everyone else who was walking. By the time we were getting close to the camp, there were more than a quarter of our original group that had died.

When we arrived at Majdanek, the first thing that we were told to do was take off our clothes so that we could wash our bodies. As there were many of us in the room, I was certain that I would not be subjected to another invasive search like when I left the experimentation room. The room that we were in was entirely made of concrete. Following the long journey, it almost was a relief to clean my body, getting rid of the smell of sweat and that stench from the camp that never seemed to leave me.

Afterward, while still naked, we were taken into a room that was pitch black. Our clothes that we had on when we arrived and put aside so that we could watch had disappeared. Our captors were intent on humiliating us as much as they could. Luckily I was not separated from Elka, and we looked at each other, with questions in our eyes, unable to will our mouths to speak. The only light we saw was from a small gap at the top of the room, left there so air could circulate. We were so many in the room that it was almost impossible to sit down. It was also hot, and we had the unpleasant sensations of our sweaty bodies bumping against each other. What made it even worse is most of the time, it was not possible to see who was next to you. Each day, we would be taken out of the room for a few minutes and dunked with cold water, and then sent back in to the dark. Before too long, people started to die all around me, some from sickness, others from what I believe was hypothermia.

If anyone cried out, or even groaned, they would be taken out and beaten. We learned to exist in the cold in silence. We were in this dark room for twelve days, and then we were taken out. By then, almost half of us had died. I was numb, dead bodies no longer scared me.

When we came out, Elka collapsed, the exhaustion taking its toll on her. I took a risk and helped her up, I needed her to survive so that I could survive. By some telepathic communication between us, she gathered what little strength she had and managed to stand up, making a concerted effort to put one foot in front of the other. Somehow, we had escaped death. Even though it was forbidden, together, we whispered a prayer of thanks.

The grim realisation of where we were began to dawn on us shortly after. Every day, we would see people coming into the camp, and we would wait for them to come out of the dark room. Most of the time, they never did. Instead, we were taken by the officials in the camp to watch, as the bodies of the dead were thrown into large holes. There, they were all burned together, as if collectively, they made up one person, rather than being the individuals that they were. Now, I realised that the other prisoners were not just Jews, there were also some Slovaks and Germans in our midst.

However, the Nazis had a way of making the entire experience of death even worse for anyone who was a Jew. When there were new Jews being brought into the camp, there would sometimes be an orchestra playing. I came to hate the sound of a full orchestra, not because I do not like music, but because of what that music represented. Usually it meant that the new arrivals were going straight to the gas chambers to be killed.

Chapter 6: Life in the Death Camp

The Nazi's would make sure that the orchestra played music that was very upbeat, and then all the new arrivals were encouraged to sing along to the music as they were marching towards the chamber. Considering the fact that most of them had endured a long and arduous journey, this was a challenging feat, although as music renews hope they tried. It was only once they were in the chamber that they realised something was amiss. As they would scream, the players in the orchestra would try and play a little louder so as to drown out the sounds.

Once I was out, I was given physical labour to do. This time I was placed in a factory, a textile factor that was making uniforms for the German soldiers. The work had a significant amount of lifting, and the air was thick with cotton particles. Although Elka was in the factory as well, she was in another section, the first time that we had not been together since we met.

In a short while, I found that I no longer had the same strength that I used to. It was taking me longer and longer to finish my tasks, and sometimes, I would not complete them as required. It was only after a week that I realised I was ill. My skin was starting to change, and often, my vision would get blurry. I wanted to do the work, yet I could not. I was sent to the infirmary, which in itself was a miracle. Most people in my condition were immediately sent to their death.

Chapter 7:

The End and the Beginning

It seemed to me that decades had gone by, but it had only been a few years. I felt old, weak and hope had escaped me. I had tried my best to fight for my life, but without hope, there was nothing for me to live for. Elka had succumbed to the challenge of living the night before, dying quietly in her sleep of starvation. I remember her courage, and being able to hold on for all that time. She was my silent partner, and now I was alone, with nothing to live for.

I had healed from my burn wounds, and although I still felt pain, it could not be compared of what it was like those first few days. Now, I was in the infirmary. I had a fever that would rage and abate at will, and my body had red spots all over. I was told that I had typhoid, so I knew my days were almost done.

The infirmary was not a place one was sent to for life, to gain back strength. It was a place where one could die quietly. There was no help or health care given, just a narrow bed where one could lie and their strength could leave them. The Germans did not like disease, and so kept away from all those who were ill until it was time to throw them in a pit with other dead bodies and cremate them.

Chapter 7: The End and the Beginning

Death was beckoning, and for me, it was a sweet calling and a welcome release. As I was in and out of consciousness, I waited for death to carry me away. I am not sure how many days went by, but I began to notice that the beds around me were empty. There were still a few who were too ill to move but for the most part, people had disappeared.

I wanted death, though I was curious as to what was happening to them. Some seemed to be getting better, and I thought that the Germans could not have decided to come in and kill them all. Why hadn't they chosen me too?

I caught the attention of one of my fellow prisoners as I tried to stagger out of bed. He said to me, "Leave now. We are Free. They are gone". I blinked, wondering if it was a dream, but he was gesturing to me, urging me to move forward, and then he disappeared. I held on to the wall and the beds as I made my way out of the room, barely able to move having gone so many days without a meal. I walked into a foreign soldier, from which country I cannot recall, who helped me walk into the light on the outside.

I was given some bread to eat and water to drink. Although I was free, I was still wary, wondering how long this would continue. I had nowhere to go, and even if I did, I could not remember how I would get there. I was free, but still imprisoned, especially in the mind. I did not know what to do.

A man came to speak to me, in a language that I did not understand. I tried to communicate but my throat would not let the words out. He found someone who could interpret and he let me know he was from America, and wanted to help. I was incredulous – it had been a long time since the word help and the thought of myself came together in the same sentence.

When I managed to take a look around me, I noticed that there were soldiers from several nations, but there were no Nazi soldiers in sight. Most of the soldiers were from the Soviet, and by looking at their faces, I could tell that they were trying to come to terms with some of the horrors that they could see.

There were prisoners like me all around, taking in deep breaths of their free air. Many of them also looked bewildered, which is the way that I felt. It was difficult to understand exactly what was happening to us. When looking at our sorry conditions, it became clear that even though we had been rescued, a large number of us, possibly even myself included, did not have that much longer to live.

Landing in America

I was again part of a large contingent of people, heading to an unknown land towards an unknown future. I remembered what it was like the first time I was taken with my mother to the ghettos. We were young then, our bodies full of strength, my hair shiny and strong, and my heart anxious about the future. Now, if you saw me, you would never believe I was that girl from yesteryears.

Like all the other prisoners that were around me I was all skin and bone. I had no fat for padding on my body, such that even when I sat down, it was my tail bone that made contact with the chair. My face was completely skeletal, and I had overheard one of the Americans referring to us as the walking dead. Indeed, that is what I resembled, and looking around me, I noticed that my fellow prisoners and I looked more like animals than like human beings.

Chapter 7: The End and the Beginning

My hair had started to grow back, though it had lost its lustre, and hung over my shoulders, thin and lank. My skin, once pearly white and smooth, was scarred, marked and rough. I had awful burn scars, and still ached on the inside. All this, and I was only 26 years old. Looking at me you may have guessed that I was in my fifties.

However, I was lucky as I had life. I was taken to live in America, to start a new life away from the trauma that I had endured. I can distinctly remember the day that I stepped foot on American soil, at Fort Ontario in New York. It was strange to look around and see no more guns, uniforms, or hear German orders. The air was free from the smell of death which still seemed to cling to my skin.

I was taken to a new home, a place where I could take the time to recover myself, mentally and physically. So much had happened in such a short time, so much had changed.

I received medical care for my wounds, and it was then that I was informed of what the X-ray machine had really done to my body. I would never have children. After all the horror I had experienced, I had lost considerable faith in the human race, so although these words were painful to hear, they were not devastating to me. I allowed myself the luxury of time, to figure out what I was to do with my life, and move forward, trying to forget the past.

Even after I made it to America, I have always wondered what became of my family, where did they all end up, and whether I have any existing relatives. For years I have hunted for them, looking for names in registers and asking other survivors whether they have come across them. For years, I have had no insight into what could have occurred.

Then, I was looking through some old photographs and I found one with my father, and one of my brothers. They were in Auschwitz camp, which was ironic as I had spent so much time there as well. In the photograph, my father and brother were standing in a line, both of them wearing their striped uniforms as was handed to all the prisoners. They had placid expressions on their faces, as if they were willing to accept whatever came their way. I know for a fact that the two of them are no longer alive. The line that they were standing in was leading to the gas chamber. I suspect they were murdered within minutes of the picture being taken.

I determined that my mother must have been murdered the same day that we both arrived at the death camp. That is what would happen to the old and the weak who were unable to defend themselves in any way. They were deemed to not be useful in society, and were therefore killed.

I still hold on to the hope that two of my brothers may be alive and looking for me somewhere in the world. As long as I do not have any evidence of their death, I must believe that they live. Maybe one day, I will be able to be with them.

In the end, I cannot escape the past, it still haunts me. I have found that sharing what happened, is the best way that I can find healing, and within myself, forgive my captors for all that they did. I continue to miss my family immensely. I have no pictures to remember them by, but their faces are imprinted in my mind. I carry the memory of their laughter in my heart, and it drives me forward.

I would like to dedicate this book to my friend Elka, who carried me, saved me and helped me stay alive to see this day.

Chapter 8:

Filling in the Gaps

Year's after I being handed my freedom and starting my new life, I found that there were so many gaps to the holocaust that I needed to fill in. Sure, I had my experiences to go by, but it seemed every person that I spoke with who was in the same situation as me had a different story to tell. I needed to satisfy my curiosity, so that I could put everything behind me.

I had always wondered why they separated me from my mother, even though she was older than I was. Other children were allowed to go with their mothers to wherever they were being taken. I had simply grown too big to qualify as her little girl. As separating mothers and their children would cause undue commotion which would have affected the efficiency with which they were eliminating the Jews, it was simple easier to keep the mothers with the children. There was no use for children anyway.

I discovered that the gas that was being used within the chambers was originally carbon monoxide. This gas was effective as it cannot be seen and it cannot be smelt. As it worked quickly, people could be dead within minutes. This gave way to the more vicious gas called Zyklon B. This gas was an insecticide, and when used on the Jews and other prisoners, there would be intense screaming as blood came pouring out of the prisoner's ears.

In the Auschwitz camp alone, which I had somehow managed to survive, more than one million people were murdered. The three camps at Auschwitz were a concentration camp, the death camp, and the labour camp.

Now I know how the Auschwitz camp operated, and how so many died even before they were able to go through all three of the sections that made up this camp. Upon arrival in Auschwitz 1, there were several places where a prisoner could be taken. There was a place known as the 'death block; the gas chamber, a crematorium and the gallows.

It was the death block that was meant to house apparent criminals, who were subject to certain court rooms where they were to be tried for all their crimes. In this place, the Jews that were captured were forced to confess to things that they had never done, through torture. Then they were sentenced to death.

Those who were sentenced at this point were not subjected to the same gas chambers as millions of other Jews. Instead, they were placed up against a wall, and they were shot at point blank range. Then their bodies were taken to the crematorium and were completely burnt.

I was oblivious of the fact that I was in the line of quick death after being asked to take out the teeth from the corpses. It turns out that most people who were given this job were eventually gassed, as the Nazis believed them to be eye witnesses. Instead of facing the gas chamber, I was transferred to another camp.

Every possible known Jewish building was destroyed during this time. This means that until 1945 from the early 1940's, there were no synagogues, Jewish businesses which number 7,000, Jewish schools and even Jewish hospitals.

The number of Jewish people who lived in Europe, and who were murdered during the holocaust totalled around 2/3 of the Jewish population at the time. This came up to 6 million at the very list, though the number of those who died is most likely around 11 million. This number does not take into account the infants as well as the babies. There were thousands of them who were murdered even before evidence of their birth could be put on record.

I was thankful that during the time my body was being experimented on, I did not come across the legendary 'Angel of Death.' He was a physician who was also based in Auschwitz, and his name was Josef Mengele. He performed the most horrific experimental procedures in patients, particularly women, children and twins. He was inhuman and by the time he was completed done with his experiments, many would have succumbed to the beckoning of death.

The Nazi's took everything from us, including all of our possessions, and even our home. After the war, the concentration camps were found to have thousands of pounds of human hair, well packaged in paper bags. I remembered my lustrous locks that had been so crudely shorn off my head.

They were using the hair to create a range of products to help them with their war efforts. The hair of the prisoners was used to create threads, which were then sown into socks. They were used when making bombs to create the ignition mechanisms. They even used our hair to create stuffing for softer mattresses. The commanders at the camp would try to meet a monthly quota. They took everything from us.

Other Horrors

Now that decades have passed, I have been able to speak to other survivors, to find out what they had gone through as well. For some, the thoughts are still so dark that they would not even mention. Others have been willing to let me know what happened to them as well.

There was a woman, Ruth, who was pregnant at the time that she was taken from her home and to the concentration camps. For some reason, they kept her alive which was odd at the time. She explained how she was kept in a room with other pregnant women, and they were given the most basic care possible until they would deliver their babies.

They helped each other with the deliveries and were only allowed to breastfeed their babies for a few days. After this, their babies were taken away from them. They then had to watch as their babies would die of starvation. Apparently, there was an experiment being carried out to find out how long a new-born baby could live without having any food.

I also met a German gentleman named Ralph, and he had also been sent to one of the concentration camps towards the end of the war. His crime had been that he was homosexual. Where Jews were forced to wear the Star of David on their shoulders as a mark of who they were, he was forced to wear a pink triangle to identify his crime. He was also experimented on, enduring what seemed like hundreds of injections each day. The only reason that he went through this torment was because he refused to consider the other options. He was told that he would have to become a prostitute, to be used freely by whoever wanted him and in whichever sexual way, or he would need to agree to be castrated. If he did either of these things, he would shortly be given his freedom.

As he refused this choice, the injections were his punishment. The Nazi physicians and scientists wanted to find out whether homosexuality was something inherited. Pumping homosexual with male hormones each day was meant to help them arrive at an answer.

Liberation

It was interesting to me to read the accounts of the people who had come to liberate us. Many of them claimed that they could not believe the horrors of what we had endured, and most questioned where we had gone wrong as humanity.

There were accounts of finding corpses piled high, as they were waiting to be buried in pits or to be cremated. Some of these corpses were yet to be searched for the gold teeth that I had learnt to extract. Most of those who were freed past away soon after, as the ravages of malnutrition as well as disease coursed through their bodies in such a way that the damage was irreparable.

To stop the spread of disease that was rife at the time, there were a large number of camps that were razed to the ground.

For a long time, I could not bring myself to accept the explanations of our liberators that they did not know what was happening to us while we were being held by the Germans. I needed to find it within me to forgive. There were not many emotions that I allowed myself to feel, but anger and disappointment were deeply rooted within me.

Chapter 8: Filling in the Gaps

It took years and reflection to believe that their words were true. I looked back at my own life. I lived in Poland for years while the war was brewing, knowing that something was amiss, but never understanding the true extent and nature of the problem. It was only after I arrived at the ghetto that the reality began to resonate within me.

Looking from the outside, all the concentration camps looked like friendly places, labour camps if you may. The signage was meant to be misleading and then there was that awful music. Anyone who would have heard it passing by, and watching the prisoners dance would have imagined that they were celebrating something joyous, and that the Nazis cared to celebrate with them. They would not have concluded that the prisoners were dancing to their death.

Deception, pain, disregard for human life and so much more is what the Nazis did to me, my family and members of my Jewish community. For many days I wanted to break as I felt that I could bend no further. For some reasons, I have survived.

Conclusion

The Holocaust marks the darkest years I have ever experienced, and I believe, the darkest years that mankind has lived through. The killing was terrible, and millions of people had their lives taken from them. I lost my whole family, not knowing whether they survived or died, but knowing that it is unlikely that I will ever see them again. The one person who I know was killed was my mother, who was sent to a gas chamber and incinerated in a pit, just because she was no longer young and strong.

Through the dangers and the journeys that I encountered living in Poland during World War 2, I learnt the value of having a friend who you could speak to without using words. The war and the concentration camps were a nightmare, though they taught me how I can speak to someone using my heart.

I still occasionally look at the tattoo on my left arm, a number that was branded on me to make me feel as though I was less than a person. Today, it is a number that reminds me I survived. Millions were captured, and millions were killed, but I was given the chance at life.

I have now created a good life for myself in the United States, and although I remember my early days in Poland with fondness, I hate to think of the days during the holocaust. I do

Conclusion

not think I will visit Poland again in my lifetime, but I do hope that my story inspires those who may have lost hope, in hope.

Made in the USA
Columbia, SC
16 March 2019